JESUS NEVER LEFT CHINA

The Rest of the Story

JESUS NEVER LEFT CHINA

The Rest of the Story

The Untold Story of the Church in China

WERNER BÜRKLIN

Foreword by Ted Engstrom

Pleasant Word (a division of WinePress Publishing, PO Box 428, Enumclaw, WA 98022) functions only as book publisher. As such, the ultimate design, content, editorial accuracy, and views expressed or implied in this work are those of the author.

ISBN 1-4141-0391-3
Library of Congress Catalog Card Number: 2005900593

Dedication

To Inge, my helpmeet for half a century, and our four children Erik, Heiko, Stephan, and Linda.

Table of Contents

Acknowledgments

First of all, my thanks go to those who prayed that this book might bless many and open the eyes of those who were confused about the facts surrounding God's work in China.

Many people along the way encouraged me to put my convictions in print. I shall always be grateful to them.

What a blessing to have had Debra Petrosky transform the writing of a German into good, readable English.

My deepest thanks go to my dear wife Inge. Without her counsel, support, and cheers, I never would have finished the project. She patiently let me do what had to be done so that God's name might be glorified.

Foreword

Having been born in China of German missionary parents, my friend Werner Bürklin has traveled to the People's Republic of China over seventy-five times during the past quarter of a century. Few Westerners are better positioned to evaluate the state of the church and its ministry in that vast nation of 1.3 billion people.

Dr. Bürklin is a missionary, evangelist, teacher, and reporter—all wrapped into one amazing individual. He has employed his expertise in all of these areas in formulating this landmark book on the state of the church in China today.

As a missionary, he has preached in churches in scores of nations across the globe over the past half century. As an evangelist, Werner served for many years with Youth for Christ and the Billy Graham Evangelistic Association, including directing the two significant International Conferences for Evangelists in Europe during his days with the association. As teacher, he has discipled hundreds of Christian leaders in China through his lectures and training sessions. As a reporter, he has insights into the evolving church scene from decades of firsthand observation.

I first met Werner when he was a young evangelist with Youth for Christ in his native Germany and have followed his career with interest. He feels passionately about the work of the Holy Spirit in China as multitudes have come to faith in our Lord Jesus Christ. Although the author expresses optimism concerning the church in China, he assesses the government's stance related to the church as well. His report highlights the powerful working of a powerful God in this burgeoning nation. God is doing amazing things in these critical days of growth and change.

I heartily commend this book to anyone who is interested in the cultural, societal, economic, political, and religious scene in that great country. Most of all, it graphically presents the face of the church in China during these days. This volume should do more than inform us, however. It should inspire all of us who long to see the gospel redeem people from every tribe, race, and nation.

I thank God for the observations our friend and author Werner Bürklin has given to us in what I consider to be a remarkable book for our time.

Ted W. Engstrom
President Emeritus
World Vision

Preface

There is more power in the open hand than in the clenched fist.

—Herbert N. Casson

This book is different.

A number of books depicting the church in China have focused on the so-called "underground church." Those stories had to be told. Since 1981, I have traveled into China over seventy-five times and enjoyed almost a quarter of a century of ministry there. During that time I have experienced a much more varied church life than has been reported by the mass media in general and the evangelical media in particular.

So much more is happening in China than what is reported. As a result, most are not aware of these changes. What sells best are negative reports, and this is a shame. Many more positive developments have taken place, and these need to be told. The *Evergreen Newsletter* of December 2004 included the following encouraging report.

Pastor Zhang, who has been a pastor in China since 1989, stated, "You can liken the church in China to the children of Israel coming out of Egypt. We're seeing miracles and the hand of God in mighty ways."

He continued, "People around the world want to focus on the problems in China. They are like the ten spies who were sent out by Moses—who returned warning of giants and great walls. Instead of listening to Caleb and Joshua, they let their fears dominate them. When God saw their lack of faith, he condemned all of Israel to wander the desert for forty years. Please tell your friends not to listen to the ten spies who tell of hardships and persecution in China. Yes, there are problems, but our God is faithful, and He is giving grace to the Chinese people! Tell people to look at China the way Joshua and Caleb looked at the Promised Land—with eyes of faith."[1]

Others share the same sentiment. Denton Lotz, general secretary of the Baptist World Alliance, wrote this:

> The apostle Paul reminds us in Philippians 4:8, "If there is anything worthy of praise, think about these things." It is indeed cause for rejoicing that the Holy Spirit is moving in China in such a marvelous way...to rejoice with those who rejoice and to tell the truth about the good things that are happening in spite of restrictions....I try to report on the good things that God is doing.[2]

I struggled to find an appropriate title for this book to focus on those good things. Humanists and human rights activists among Christians rightfully exposed the dark side of the communist regime as told in multiple stories on persecution. Another side to the evolving political establishment in China exists, however. This is not only reflected in China's economic boom but also in the government's aggressive steps to advance the legal system. Eventually this will affect the interpretation of the religious freedom article of the Chinese constitution. The effects are already being felt. The latter

---

[1] *Evergreen Newsletter,* December 2004, Evergreen Family Friendship Service, Colorado Springs, CO 80919.

[2] *Religious Herald,* September 16, 2004, Richmond, Virginia.

has not been adequately reported. I wanted to reflect this in the title of this book.

Ruth Graham, in a letter she wrote to me regarding China, gave me an idea. She quoted Paul Harvey's motto, "and now the rest of the story . . ." from his famous radio show. The western media circulated so many controversial news stories—some of them true, but the majority of them misleading—that I felt compelled to relate "the rest of the story" of China. What had annoyed me most? The never-ending flow of stories of persecuted Christians left the impression that every Christian in China is being persecuted or under siege, and that is not so. To the contrary, millions worship Christ freely. Of course human rights violations exist. But have we forgotten the government's effort to implement policies of religious freedom?

The first title to come to my mind was "Jesus in China: The Rest of the Story." To make sure that this would be agreeable to David Aikman, who had titled his book *Jesus in Beijing*, I shared my intention with him. I purposely have not read his book so as not to be influenced by his opinions. He responded swiftly and decisively, asking me not to use it.

Then I came across a title used by Stanley Karnow in the final pages of *Life and Death in Shanghai*.[3] His title was *Mao and China*.[4] Karnow depicts the legacy of Mao, a brutal man who plunged China into fear and mental enslavement. He became a tyrannical emperor like others before him. Since his death, however, a new China has emerged. Religions were reinstated, and for the first time in centuries, Christianity is being embraced as well. So I toyed with the title "Jesus and China: The Rest of the Story" because Jesus is now in the hearts of millions of Chinese. I wanted to focus on Jesus and His followers in China.

---

[3] Nien Cheng, *Life and Death in Shanghai* (New York: Penguin Books, 1988), 531.

[4] Stanley Karnow, *Mao and China: A Legacy of Turmoil* (New York: Penguin Books, 1985).

A pastor in Shanghai told me a story that clinched my search for a title. Overjoyed by this pastor's invitation to perform in his church, the members of a singing group from the United States composed a song specifically for this occasion. They stood in front of the congregation and enthusiastically sang, "How wonderful for Jesus to have returned to China." The pastor appreciated their enthusiasm but then pulled them aside after the service and said, "Thank you so much for your gusto, but listen—Jesus never left China." This led me to the title I now use. Indeed Jesus had never left China!

The Chinese government has restricted spiritual expressions to five major religions: Buddhism, Taoism, Islam, Catholicism, and Protestantism. Being a Protestant, and having worked exclusively within that body, I want to limit my observations and experiences of church life to that part of believers.

According to the ruling authorities in China, Protestant Christians fall into two major groupings: the registered and the unregistered church. The West depicts them as state churches and underground churches. But neither an underground church nor a state church exists in China. England has a state church with the queen as the head of the Anglican Church, but no similar institution exists in China with its communist government. The Chinese government does recognize a legal and an illegal church, however.

Many of the so-called underground churches are very visible and mostly tolerated by the authorities. Therefore you cannot label them as underground churches. They don't meet in caves (except in areas of China where caves are also used as dwelling places) and "behind bushes." In no way are they underground like the early Christians were, who worshiped in catacombs in order to escape oppressive Roman rule and often had to face the lions in amphitheaters. In a totalitarian country like China it is impossible to operate churches clandestinely. Thousands of them function.

Most China observers would agree that never before and in no other country has the Christian community grown so fast as in the Middle Kingdom right now.

Beginning with the modern missionary movement in the nineteenth century, thousands of missionaries from across the western world served faithfully and diligently in China. Many of them, and some of them with their children, lie buried in its soil. When Mao Zedong rose as the victorious leader in 1949, however, a new challenge faced the Christian church.

As a Westerner my interpretation of events may differ from those of people living in China, but in no way are they meant to criticize in any way those who hold different views. To the contrary, I have learned much from my many friends in China. I am deeply grateful to them.

Let me take you on an exciting journey. The supposed death rattle of the church in China has been transformed into a dynamic force of an emerging faith that has swept across a land formerly blocked to the spreading of the gospel of Jesus Christ. On October 1, 1949, when Mao Zedong declared on Tiananmen Square, "China finally stood up," this became true for the church in China as well. The so-called "opiate for the people" turned into a pulsating life-blood for the nation.

Chapter 1

Going Home

"What in the world are you doing here?"

I sat on the platform of a tiny train station somewhere deep in China, reading my German Bible. A Chinese man with a fragile build approached me. He seemed to be in his early thirties. His eyes squinted in the sun as he peered at me, waiting for an answer. He probably hadn't seen many foreigners in this remote area. His delicate fingers leafed through my Bible.

"Is that a dictionary?" he asked.

His English was excellent, but he did not know any German. An agent with the China travel service, he immediately contacted the local authorities. I wondered what would happen to me next. Would I be detained or permitted to travel to my destination?

How Did I Get There?

In 1981, I had called the Chinese embassy in Bonn, Germany, for permission to travel to my former home in China. "No, you cannot travel to Jiangxi," said the official. Jiangxi, the province where my parents had labored as missionaries in the 1920s, 1930s, and 1940s, was also known as the "revolution province."

In 1931, Mao Zedong had established the first Soviet Republic in the mountains (Jinggan-shan) of the southern part of that province, encompassing some 10,000,000 people. But three years later his opponent Chiang Kai-shek forced him to go on his epic trek called the Long March with 85,000 of his troops and 15,000 administrative personnel. It was a rout. Only about 10,000 survived.[5] Close to the Mongolian border they established their new headquarters in Yanan in the province of Shanxi.

I wanted to return to the country of my birth. I wanted to get back to my roots. I longed to see the river where I used to swim. I wanted to revisit Cui Wei Feng, the rocky hill where young communists who wanted to establish a new egalitarian society in China had liquidated a host of landowners. I wanted to see my old home, which had been built in the early twentieth century.

Recently Deng Xiaoping had opened China's doors to the western world. To his critics who felt that bad influences would enter the nation, he said, "We need fresh air, taking the risk of bad flies as well." He had embarked on a new policy of rapprochement. But the government left the province of Jiangxi closed to foreigners. The provincial leaders, hard-core communists, had not forgotten the bloody revolution. They called it liberation.

I entered the Chinese embassy in Bonn, Germany. Chinese construction workers had just completed it. They did not want Germans to build it. They did not trust them. Weren't bugs planted in such facilities? Laborers from China had to do the job.

Not wanting to take no for an answer, I decided to visit the embassy in person. I hoped to find a more sympathetic official than the one I had spoken to over the phone. Perhaps someone here would help me return to my home in China.

---

[5] One author estimates as many as 20,000 to 40,000 may have survived. James C. F. Wang, *Contemporary Chinese Politics: an Introduction* (Englewood Cliffs, NJ: Prentice Hall, 1995), 19, 181.

An Unexpected Opportunity

I met the head of the cultural department of the embassy. This petite, attractive, and well-groomed lady was not clothed in the typical Mao suit. After greeting me warmly, she immediately asked a question.

"What is a church?"

Her question stunned me. She must have done her homework. How else did she know that I was an ordained minister? Or did she?

"I come from Beijing," she continued. "I have been here for two months. While exploring the countryside, I noticed big buildings with steeples. Are those churches?"

"Yes, those are churches. But the real church is made up of people who follow Jesus Christ," I replied.

"Who is Jesus Christ?" she asked.

No doubt this intelligent lady had heard about Jesus. Officials who work in an embassy are well versed in the culture of the land in which they serve. I sensed she wanted to know more about Him besides what she had learned during her university studies.

Someone who had so many followers intrigued her. Close to two billion people worldwide claim to be Christians. Christianity had spread to the remotest corners of the world, outnumbering Judaism from which it had sprung. In the beginning only twelve followed Him. Those were His disciples, later called apostles. But why were those followers willing to stand up for a person who had been crucified as Mel Gibson portrayed in his blockbuster movie *Passion of the Christ*? Judas, the betrayer, hung himself. All but one of the remaining disciples had died brutal deaths as well. They had been tortured, stoned, beaten, imprisoned, or crucified. According to legend, outspoken Peter was crucified upside down. But others took their place and made Christianity the largest religion of the world.

Even China had Christians now, multitudes of them. Many had lost their lives during the Great Proletarian Cultural Revolution (from now on referred to as the Cultural Revolution).

The Cultural Revolution, the darkest period of the Mao regime, can be summarized in *Life and Death in Shanghai,* a vivid account by Nien Cheng about her six and a half years in solitary confinement.

> Mao had declared, "The Proletarian Cultural Revolution is a great political revolution of the proletarian class against the capitalist class. It is the continuation of the class struggle by the proletarian class against the capitalist class. It is also the continuation of the class struggle by the Communist Party against Kuomintang."[6]

The Red Guards, mostly fanatical young people brainwashed by "Mao Zedong thought," sought to destroy anyone perceived as not being loyal to their leader. Nien Cheng's cook described their viciousness in this firsthand account:

> "You can't imagine what Shanghai was like in 1967 and 1968," said the cook. "The Red Guards and the Revolutionaries went mad. They ran wild in the city, looting and abducting people at will, torturing them in secret courts, and killing them in every cruel way imaginable. It wasn't safe for anyone to go out on the streets. They even used ambulances to abduct people when there weren't enough vehicles for their purposes. There were so many suicides! And many people went to the police stations begging to be taken to prison for protection."

Now I sat in the Chinese embassy, talking to a lady who also had gone through the infamous Cultural Revolution and expressed interest in Jesus Christ.

---

[6] Nien Cheng, *Life and Death in Shanghai* (New York: Penguin Books, 1988), 286.

Why would so many people follow the teachings of Jesus, who had lived and died some two thousand years ago and apparently had been a failure? She really wanted to know. For the next ninety minutes we talked about Him.

"Do you think the church can change man?" she asked.

"No, the church cannot, but Jesus can," I replied. Immediately I thought of Mao Zedong whose goal had been to change man. In the process he enslaved an entire nation, but people did not change for the better. No wonder she was intrigued by Jesus who not only changed man but also altered history. She wanted to find the truth.

"Just Sign Up With A Tour Group"

While I enjoyed our conversation, I also had come to get a visa. "Yes, you may visit Shanghai, Beijing, Guangzhou, or any of the main cities in China," she said. "Just sign up with a tour group." But that was the last thing I wanted to hear. I was not interested in tourist sites. I wanted to go home.

She sensed my frustration. "I will send a telex to Guangzhou." She tried to comfort me with the extra effort. "The authorities there might help you. I cannot."

Guangzhou, formerly known as Canton, is a large city located some ninety miles north of Hong Kong. I took a speedboat from Hong Kong following the Pearl River. A young Chinese met me at the pier. Claiming to be a tourist guide, he offered to show me Guangzhou. I wondered whether the authorities had sent him to keep an eye on me. During those years few foreigners ventured into China, and the authorities were suspicious of them. But I did not care. I wanted to go home.

"Please take me to the immigration office," I requested.

"Why?"

"A telex is waiting for me there."

This nice young man accommodated my wishes and did not argue. Once we arrived, the officials promptly informed me that I had come in vain.

"There is no telex for you. We don't even have telex machines in our offices."

"I'm going back to Hong Kong," I told my new friend as I retrieved my passport.

"Oh, no!" he exclaimed. "You have come to see China!"

Yes, I had, but the China I wanted to see was not on any tourist trip. I left the immigration office, caught a train in Guangzhou, and headed toward a remote part of China. Twelve hours later, when I recognized the province where my parents had worked, I jumped off the train. That's when the agent at the train station detained me. As we headed to the police station, I reminisced about my boyhood home.

Remembering China

I thought of the river in Nanfeng, the city where I had lived. My mother never wanted me to swim in it. "They clean their chamber pots in that river, in fact in all rivers across China. I don't want you to get sick," she exhorted. As teenagers we didn't care. We wanted to swim.

My parents had three children, one girl and two boys. All of us had gone through some severe sicknesses. My sister's life once hung delicately on a thread. When Gisela[7] was seven years old, she almost died. Pneumonia was hard to cure in those years without competent doctors and the right kind of medicine. I had gone through the severest bout of malaria. It was the worst of three stages. I almost

---

[7] She later changed her name to Joy—a direct translation from her Chinese name. My brother Friedel also changed his name to Frederick. I kept my German name.

did not make it. A Chinese doctor had rushed to my bedside, but he could not help. My parents prayed and I pulled through.

As an infant my older brother Friedel had saved my mother's life and his own by hollering at the top of his voice. My father had put them both on a tiny sampan to escape the oncoming marauding and vicious communist insurgents. "I can't travel with a sick infant. My heart breaks listening to his screams!" my mother sobbed. So my father took them back to the mission station. Three other Scandinavian missionary ladies departed on that same boat and were never heard from again.

No matter what my mother said, we wanted to swim. There were no swimming pools in those days, not in Jiangxi, and definitely not in Nanfeng. So we swam in the polluted river Fu Hejiang. Once we took a friend along. I was sixteen; he was much younger. The river had many sand banks. Shallow water covered some of them, making it treacherous to play in those areas. My brother and I weren't lifeguards, but we knew how to swim.

We heard a cry. Our small friend, who couldn't swim, had lost his footing and fell into the deep. Seeing him bobbing up and down, we rushed to pull him out. He choked and spat water as he gasped for air. No wonder my mother did not want us to swim in the river. I thought of the chamber pots. But we gladly came to our friend's rescue.

When we arrived home shaken, his father greeted us, asking, "What happened? While you were out, I had a strange feeling that something had gone wrong. All I could do was pray." God had answered his prayers.

More memories flooded my mind. I also thought about those landowners on the rock called Cui Wei Feng. The communists did not like rich people. Landowners were known to lord it over peasants—and Mao had come to liberate the peasants. In the process he had murdered many landowners. A number of the landowners sought refuge on top of a rock that could be scaled only through a cliff on one side. For several weeks they found refuge there, but then food and water ran out. Promised safe passage if they would hand over their property, the landowners climbed down one by one. Because of the steep, narrow cliff, they could not see each other. As the landowners reached the bottom, the communists beheaded them one by one. Only a few of them were spared. I never could suppress such memories.

Now I faced another communist.

Interrogation

The head of the police department sat behind a table. He was dressed like Mao. All Chinese were dressed alike. We called them "blue ants." We called those who wore gray suits the "gray ants." Perhaps the gray ants had a higher rank. But I did not care. The chief of police lectured me on what I could and could not do. One forbidden thing was getting off a train in the middle of China. Several policemen watched as I tried to explain why I had jumped off the train.

"I wanted to go home," I replied. This startled him.

"What do you mean, 'go home'?"

"I used to live here."

"How come?"

"My parents lived here," I replied.

I felt a little uneasy. Perspiration dampened my collar. The worst he could do was imprison me for a few days, I reasoned. Then they would let me go and call me *persona non grata*. But I did not want my wife to read about this in the newspapers. Inge had gone through everything with me. But I feared this would be too much for her.

I had heard that communists were tough, but my interrogator was surprisingly courteous. I guess he kind of liked me. *Not too many foreigners would jump off a train in the middle of China,* he must have thought. *This guy is weird.* He wanted to know more about me, and his questions were relentless.

"So your parents lived here," the uniformed commander ventured. "What in the world did they do here?"

The agent who had picked me up on that wretched railroad station had asked a similar question: "What in the world are you doing here?"

To understand why I had jumped off a train in the middle of China, you have to understand my family's history.

My Parents Met In China

My parents were German citizens. Gustav Bürklin was born in Mannheim, Lina Pfeifferling on a farm in a beautiful region of central Germany. Both of them wanted to serve God in China. He graduated from St. Chrischona, a theological seminary in Switzerland. She studied nursing in Kassel, near her home. They met each other on the mission field. He had seen a picture of her in a Christian magazine hosting small children at a party. *A person who likes children would make a good wife,* he mused. But they lived hundreds of miles apart. In those days people traveled by foot or by river houseboats. Wanting to get to know that warmhearted lady with the kids, he commenced his long journey.

His heart beat faster when he finally arrived in the little town of Linchuan. His Chinese traveling companion must have been a seasoned carrier of heavy loads, sturdy and strong. He used a bamboo pole across his shoulder to balance and lighten the load. On treacherous footpaths along rice fields or through rapids in rivers you needed someone to help carry your bags or guide you from shore to shore. He walked through the narrow streets in Linchuan. Storekeepers stared at this "foreign devil," as foreigners were called. The Chinese saw few white faces with long noses in the backwoods of their country in those days. In contrast to the Chinese, my father had a long nose, but he was handsome.

The locals also called aliens "tigers." They smelled differently, like wild beasts, the small-nosed residents decided. Showers were not available, in fact not known. But other things smelled more offensive to my father. Open gutters released the stench of sewers. Garlic drifted through the air. Sunburned farmers returned from the field with their swaying black water buffalos. Saliva dripped from the animals' nostrils, not a pleasant sight to watch. Children swarmed the stranger and kept chanting, "Foreign devil!" The toddlers wore slit pants and simply squatted to relieve themselves. As he made his way to the *Libai Tang*, or worship hall, as the church was known, he undoubtedly prayed that God would lead him as He had led Jacob to find favor with Rachel whom he eventually married.

"You have come in vain," the senior missionary, a kind man, told him.

After such a long journey those words took my father's breath away. Miss Pfeifferling had been transferred to Nancheng, a city forty miles further south—another two days of strenuous walking.

"Nach Gutem muss man laufen," the missionary said in German. Keep on walking to find the good you are looking for. But before moving on, my father needed some rest. Someone brought him a bowl of hot water, and with a flimsy washcloth he wiped sweat from his brow and armpits. He enjoyed the hot green tea offered to him.

Eventually Gustav and Lina met, married, and shared in their missionary enterprise together. They had three children in quick succession, and I was the middle one.

The Moment Of Truth

"What in the world did they do here?" the police chief pressed me once more.

"My parents were missionaries," I told him.

I hadn't returned to China as someone who wanted to sneak around. Even before entering China, I had decided to be honest and open and to follow the laws of the land. After all, I had been born in China. China was my motherland. I identified with the citizens of this proud and ancient land, even though I disliked the communists, at least at that time. I simply wanted to go home.

I had one trump card left—an identity card that had been issued when we lived in Jiangxi. The police chief examined it closely. It contained Chinese characters with my Chinese name and the address where I had lived. He smiled as he studied the photo of a sixteen-year-old. Many years had passed since it was taken. He showed it to one of the policemen who stood nearby. Getting up from behind his desk, the police chief walked toward me. While shaking my hand, he said, "Welcome home." Within three hours I had a special permit to visit every town and village I wanted to see.

I was home.

Chapter 2

Eleven O'clock at Night

Night had fallen when I arrived in Nancheng, which is located in the center of the Jiangxi province. My father had met my mother in this town early in the twentieth century. After having visited this place on my first trip to China in March 1981, I was back again.

"Go To The River"

On my first trip I had looked for the mission station, but no one could locate it for me. Nobody I had asked knew where foreigners had lived so many years ago. But this time I wanted to find it. When I had returned to Germany from my first trip to China, an old missionary who had served with my parents counseled, "Go to the river." Missionaries often sought real estate that bordered on rivers. Rivers served as highways in those days.

Most of the streets in Nancheng did not have any electric light. I found my way to the riverbank with difficulty. Often only the moon lit my path. It was nearly eleven o'clock at night.

Women washed their clothes in the river—just like they had done when we lived in China forty years earlier. Others bathed, and still others brushed their teeth. I remembered my swimming feats and the chamber pots when I was young. Now an adult, I would never swim in such dirty waters.

The former missionary had pointed me to the river to find the mission station. But where was the European-style building with a wraparound verandah? As I trudged up the steps from the riverbank, a Chinese man approached me. I did not recognize him. Bringing his face within ten inches of mine, he studied my features. Feeling uncomfortable with his intrusion, I quickly skirted around him.

"Are you the son of Lin Le De?" he called out.

His question stunned me. I could not believe that someone in the middle of China recognized me. How did he know my father's Chinese name?

All early missionaries adopted Chinese names and often wore Chinese clothes. Missionaries with the China Inland Mission even wore pigtails just like most men did during the Qing Dynasty, also called the Manchu Dynasty (1644–1911). They wanted to identify with the people among whom they lived and with whom they worked.

"What should my name be?" my father asked the man chosen to find the proper Chinese name for him.

"Please pronounce your name," the name specialist offered.

"Bürklin."

"That's easy!" he exclaimed. "Your Chinese name will be Lin. This is a good common surname in our land. We'll simply drop the first syllable."

When I was born, I also was given a Chinese name. I am known as Lin Ming Dan in China.

But that night, the Chinese on the riverbank called out my father's name. I could not believe what I heard. How would anyone in China still know Lin Le De? I whirled around and faced him.

"Yes, Lin is my father. But how do you know who I am? How do you know that I am the son of Lin Le De? How did you recognize me?"

"Don't you remember me?" he asked excitedly. "I was your parents' cook!"

RECOGNIZED IN NANFENG

On my first trip to China in early 1981, I had visited the towns where my parents had done missionary work—including Nancheng. But this episode had started in Nanfeng, a town further south. Because I was the first foreigner who had returned after the Cultural Revolution, hundreds of people followed me wherever I went. Most people living there had never seen a foreigner. A few of the older citizens had but not the new generation. A tall Caucasian with a long nose attracted everyone's attention. The whole town came out in droves to see me.

"Where is the former mission station?" I had asked the officials who had welcomed me warmly. They did not know what I was talking about.

"Are there Christians in this town?"

"No, they were all liquidated during the Cultural Revolution," they answered.

In desperation I asked them to find an old person who might remember missionaries. Hundreds followed me as I was taken to a ramshackle home. I stooped low to fit through the door. A wrinkled old lady greeted me in the darkened room. She must have been in her nineties. After the initial shock of seeing a foreigner enter her abode, she smiled widely.

"Yes, I remember foreigners living in this town many years ago!" she exclaimed. "They lived in the *Jasu Tang*." In the dialect of that region, *Jasu* means Jesus. She referred to the Jesus Hall, so off we went to the *Jasu Tang*.

I had to wade through the crowds as they surged forward to face me. It reminded me of Moses passing through the Red Sea. How long had it been since this town had seen a Caucasian? With no television in this area, my arrival had generated both news and entertainment.

Hundreds of people stood at the gate as my escorts led me into the former mission compound—now a fire brigade station. The government had confiscated all religious buildings during the Cultural Revolution. They transformed them into warehouses, public halls, factories, storage places, and meeting places. You name it, they found some nonreligious use for them.

Unknown to me, one of those onlookers was a Christian. Too scared to identify himself as such, he wrote to his friend in Nancheng, our former cook, "The son of former missionaries has returned. Can you believe that?"

The cook I had known then was sixteen years old. He had been a likable fellow, easy in his laugh. He had joked with us a lot. Thirty-five years later, now in his early fifties, he looked as if he had endured hard times. He beamed an engaging smile from his toughened countenance. He had found an old friend.

He dragged me to his dwelling—two shabby-looking rooms. One was totally empty. He explained that he had cleaned it for my mother.

"I thought your mother would accompany you," he said. "I remember her to be an extremely clean lady. Everything had to be spick and span all the time. So I cleaned as best as I could. Meiyou Wanze," he laughed.

Meiyou in Chinese means no, and *Wanze* in German means bedbug. *He even remembered some German,* I mused. China had millions of bedbugs when we lived there. They were called "China's millions." Before praying with us, my father often recited a rhyme when he put us to bed: "Good night, sleep tight, don't let the bedbugs bite. If they do, take your shoe and slap those nasty things in two."

Our cook proudly announced that now China had eliminated all *Wanzen* within its borders.

"But tell me how you found me. How did you recognize me—especially in the middle of the night?"

"When you visited Nanfeng a few months ago, hundreds of people followed you," he explained. "One of them, a Christian friend of mine, wrote me that you had returned to China. Then you wrote a letter to the innkeeper of this town. No one in our city ever receives letters from Germany. The innkeeper had it translated into Chinese by a middle school teacher. This letter became the news of the town. You had written that you would come back during August. I gathered that you would visit the mission station where you had lived. Starting on the first day of August, I walked up and down the riverbank near the old mission station, hoping and praying that we would meet."

We met around eleven o'clock at night on August 28, 1981. He had waited twenty-eight long days. God had brought us together.

From Cook To Shepherd

"What do you now do?" I inquired.

"I am the shepherd of a flock. It is a small group of believers."

"How is this possible? How can you be a shepherd?" I exclaimed. "You were a cook. You have never gone to seminary, not even a Bible school."

"But I heard your father preach. I remember the Bible stories he told us. So that is what I passed on. I don't have a Bible. In fact, I still don't have one. I have to rely on my memory. The government confiscated and destroyed all Bibles and New Testaments during the dark days of the Cultural Revolution."

"Where and how do you meet?" I was curious.

"We meet in homes."

"What kind of services do you have?"

"First I tell them a Bible story and relate that to the gospel. Then I ask people to give testimonies about what God has done in their lives during the past week. I don't want testimonies about what happened long ago. I want fresh stories from my flock. That fills another hour. It is hard for them to quit. After that we pray. That takes up most of the time."

It was late, so I returned to the inn. I asked our former cook to come back at seven o'clock in the morning. Eager to reminisce, I looked forward to more fellowship with him.

The next morning I went down to the gate to meet him.

"My former cook is coming to see me," I told the innkeeper. "I asked him to arrive at seven o'clock, but he still is not here."

The innkeeper looked at me sternly.

"He was here at six o'clock, but I sent him away. Remember, you have come to visit the sights. You have not come to see old friends."

His rebuke devastated me. Yes, this happened shortly after the Cultural Revolution.

The Cultural Revolution was a dreadful time for all of China. Nien Cheng explained it this way:

> While the Great Proletarian Revolution was different things to different people, this gigantic struggle lasting ten full years was essentially a contest between two conflicting Party policies personified by Mao Zedong and Liu Shaoqui [Liu was chairman of the Chinese People's Republic]. The irony is that although Mao Zedong had Lui Shaoqui persecuted to death and seemed to have won during the Cultural Revolution, after his own death, Deng Xiaoping led China along the route of economic liberalization pioneered by Liu Shaoqui twenty years earlier, and went much further than anybody in China or the rest of the world could possibly have imagined during the days of the Cultural Revolution.[8]

The government had banned foreigners from visiting the interior of this revolution province and fraternizing with its citizens. I had been let in as a special favor. I wanted to call the chief of police in the capital city of Jiangxi, but I refrained. I knew I would be treading on treacherous ground. China was still closed to the outside world—at least at that time.

---

[8] Nien, *Life and Death in Shanghai,* 209.

I never saw my newfound friend again. Later I heard that he had died a natural death soon after our reunion.

Chapter 3

Caught up in China's Gulag

Tyranny is always better organized than freedom.

—Péguy

James Hudson Taylor founded the China Inland Mission. Dixon E. Hoste succeeded him as general director. Then George W. Gibb took the helm until Bishop Frank Houghton assumed leadership in 1940. After World War II every Friday evening the bishop stood in front of a small group of Shanghai teenagers and taught the Bible at the Free Christian Church. He loved young people—and I was one of them. A true mentor, he sent me handwritten letters of encouragement and admonition until his death.

Henry was also one of those teenagers. Born in Hawaii on December 16, 1926, he returned to his homeland in 1932 along with his Chinese mother and father. He was a quiet, shy but dedicated young man when he joined our group, the Ambassadors for Christ. Desiring to lift his people out of disease and poverty, he studied medicine. As a young surgeon he worked at the Eastern Shanghai Hospital, but then the political situation changed.

Swept Away By The Communist Revolution

Having been brought up in a forward-looking family, Henry was not content with the belligerent propaganda the new regime offered. The leaders talked about building a new society, but instead they enslaved the people by putting their minds in chains. Wanting to be free, Henry listened on the radio to the Voice of America and the BBC, which the government had forbidden. Despite the risk, he yearned for news of events in the rest of the world. One day law enforcement agents rushed into his home, demanding, "Turn off that radio! You are under arrest."

One of his friends had betrayed him.

"Why do you go against the law? You are a spy!" his interrogators accused him. "You know it is prohibited to listen to your enemies."

"I am not a spy."

"But you are engaged in activities that are harmful to our country. Foreign radio broadcasts will defile your mind."

"How can that be?" Henry insisted. "My parents lived in Hawaii, where I was born, but chose to return to the land they loved. They taught me to love my country and build up the nation. What is wrong about finding out how people live in other countries? Furthermore, I am a Christian and only want to do what is honorable. So was Sun Yatsen[9] whom you admire. Look at his statue in the center of Nanjing and at the pompous mausoleum on the hill."

"We despise Christianity! Marx taught that religion is the opiate of the people. So did Lenin."

Being a Christian and listening to foreign radio broadcasts landed him first in prison and then in a labor camp in the province of Anhui.

---

[9] Dr. Sun Yatsen was a Christian and had been educated in Western schools in Hawaii and Hong Kong; his rather crude political theories, which envisioned a new China, founded on what he termed the Three Principles—Nationalism, Democracy, and People's Livelihood—were largely derived from Western political and social thinkers. John A. Garrity and Peter Gay, eds., *The Columbia History of the World* (New York: Harper & Row, Publishers), 943.

Those were dreadful years. Among hundreds of others, he was forced to do hard labor. He slept body to body in shacks. "In the winter some of my friends froze to death, and in the summer the heat sapped us of all strength," he told me.

We had not heard from each other in decades. Henry had no contact with his old Shanghai friends or with anyone outside of China for thirty-three years. While I pursued a wonderful career, he languished in prison-like surroundings for twenty-three long years.

And then an amazing thing happened.

Finding Henry

Released from imprisonment in 1980, Henry was banished to Paoting, a city south of Beijing with a population of more than 100,000. He was forced to work as an interpreter in one of the many state industrial units. Friends in Hong Kong helped me to track him down.

In 1984, I had just finished my assignment with the Billy Graham Evangelistic Association. I had the vision of sharing what we had learned at Amsterdam '83[10] with Chinese evangelists. While exploring this endeavor, I would visit with Henry in Paoting, if possible. Reuniting with an old acquaintance was tougher than I had anticipated, however.

My wife and I landed in Shanghai. We checked into the Broadway Mansion Hotel across from the Suzhou Creek, one of the very few foreign hotels left from pre-Mao days. In a letter I had asked Henry to meet me there, but this was impossible for him to do. I began to learn how difficult it was for the Chinese to travel within their own country. They also did not have the money to make extended trips.

---

[10] Billy Graham sponsored an International Conference for Itinerant Evangelists, the first of three such conferences. Others were Amsterdam '86 and Amsterdam 2000.

So we traveled on. We delivered several Moody Science films to the Jingling Theological Seminary in Nanjing. We had hoped that Henry would contact us there, and he did. In a telegram he urged us to come to Paoting.

The sun beat down on us as we disembarked at the run-down railroad station. Paoting is certainly not a tourist spot. As we pushed forward alongside our fellow-travelers to find the exit, a railroad employee spotted us and immediately steered us to the outlet for privileged people. At least that is how they made us feel. We were the only privileged ones on that train.

Masses of people flooded the square facing the railroad station. Everywhere you go in China this seems to be the case. Over one billion Chinese inhabitants crowd its cities, towns, and villages. No wonder people are everywhere! But how would we find Henry?

Henry found us first. A large straw hat covered his head as he slowly moved toward us. He looked so old. Years of hard labor had worn down his body, giving him a frail appearance. His delicate fingers, which used to handle surgical instruments and scalpels, now looked like stumps on his hands.

"Are you Werner?" he whispered while throngs of onlookers crowded around us. In the early 1980s foreigners did not travel to remote areas. Many Chinese probably had never seen a Caucasian. And what would one of their own have to do with a foreigner?

We sat down in the overcrowded waiting room. Spotting us again, the railroad employee opened the VIP room. Finally we could talk in privacy and without fear. In those days we were not sure whether such encounters could harm our Chinese friends.

Henry's eyes reflected sadness and fear. "Chinese 'CIA agents'[11] are everywhere," he cautioned. "I don't trust anyone. I love China with its beautiful landmarks, unique architecture, unparalleled silk, cloisonné, and curiosities. But I cannot forget the pain the system

[11] He was referring to China's State Security Bureau.

inflicted upon me. True, it has improved lately, but they cannot erase what is engraved in my memory."

His suffering had made Henry a lonely, wounded man. After all of those horrendous experiences throughout the prime of his life, he now lived in a place totally removed from his loved ones. His parents had died during the Cultural Revolution. His close friends lived overseas. No family, no wife, no Christian fellowship, no Bible, no church to attend. He was all alone and broken in spirit. A wasted life like countless others in an oppressive land?

Henry is one of the heroes of faith described in Hebrews 11.

> Who through faith subdued kingdoms, wrought righteousness, obtained promises, stopped the mouths of lions, quenched the violence of fire, escaped the edge of the sword, out of weakness were made strong, waxed valiant in fight, turned to flight armies of the aliens. Women received their dead raised to life again: and others were tortured, not accepting deliverance; that they might obtain a better resurrection: and others had trials of cruel mocking and scourging, yea, moreover of bonds and imprisonment: they were stoned, they were sawn asunder, were tempted, were slain with the sword: they wandered about in sheepskins and goatskins; being destitute, afflicted, tormented; of whom the world was not worthy: they wandered in deserts, and in mountains, and in dens and caves of the earth. And these all, having obtained a good report through faith, received not the promise.[12]

Our faith does not merely deliver us out of difficulty. Chinese Christians know the grace that sustains them in the midst of trials. This was Henry's testimony. Because of all his suffering in this life, he will enjoy his heavenly reward that much more.

Henry was just one of the persecuted Christians I met on my travels to China. After the Cultural Revolution ended, I met other believers who had also suffered for their faith.

---

[12] Hebrews 11:33–39 KJV.

Chapter 4

Brainwashed Yet Faithful

In revolution there is no joy. *Nor ever will be.*

—Rozinov

Five years after the Cultural Revolution not much had changed in China. The government and its people had only begun to recover from the shock of those ten dark years that no living Chinese will ever forget. Families had been torn apart. No one trusted the next person. Corruption and mismanagement ran rampant. Everyone looked out for himself. The task of rebuilding the country would be possible only by lifting the spirit of the people. The government had lost credibility.

The main perpetrators of the Cultural Revolution—the Gang of Four—were now in prison, however. This was an important, if not earthshaking, development. A few years before, no one in China could have imagined the turn of events. All eyes were now on the Four. One of them was Mao's third wife, Jiang Qing; the others were Wang Hongwen, Zhang Chungqiao, and Yao Wenyuan, a well-known left-wing writer, all prominent leaders in China at that time. Before 1966, the beginning of the Cultural Revolution, all four were low-ranking officials but later manipulated the young people who were known as the Red Guards.

Mao's Third Wife

Even Mao's wife did not have much clout in the early years of their marriage. Born in Chu Cheng in Shandong province, she had been raised by her grandfather. She became an actress and an early left-wing revolutionary. In 1933, the Kuomintang authorities imprisoned her for her activities in a communist front organization. Upon her release in Shanghai, she continued her career as a left-wing actress but escaped to Chongqing when the Japanese occupied the Hankou district of Shanghai in 1937.

Her political convictions drove her to the communist stronghold that had been established by Mao and his followers in Yanan, Shanxi province, in northern China. There she met the chairman of the communist party and fell in love with him. In 1930, the Kuomintang executed Mao's first wife[13], after which he had married Ho Tzu-chen, the woman he had been living with for two years. While Mao's second wife underwent treatment in a Moscow hospital, Jiang Qing became his third wife. They married against the wishes of many top party members, who made her promise to stay out of politics for thirty years.

Dr. Li Zhisui, the personal physician of Mao, had this to say in his book *The Private Life of Chairman Mao:*

> Jiang Qing had made her first public appearance on September 29, two days after the close of the Tenth Plenum. The occasion was a meeting with the wife of Indonesia's president Sukarno, and a photograph of the event, the first of Mao's wife ever published, appeared in the *People's Daily* the next day...Jiang Qing's public appearance aroused widespread public attention. It was a violation of the longstanding prohibition against her involvement in politics.[14]

---

[13] At the age of fourteen, Mao was married to a girl six years older only known as "Woman Luo." Mao said of her "I do not consider her my wife." Jung Chang and Jon Halliday, *Mao: the unknown story* (New York: Random House, 2005), 7

[14] Dr. Li Zhisui, *The Private Life of Chairman Mao* (New York: Random House, 1994), 401.

In reality, Jiang Qing was a very insecure woman. Dr. Li described her in not very flattering terms.

> She lived a life of luxury. Everything she wanted, she was given. But she had nothing to do. Her life had no meaning. Jiang Qing was adrift. Mao was both busy and indifferent to her, and she no longer shared his life. There was a twenty-year gap between them, and their tastes and preferences were completely different. Jiang Qing insisted on schedule and routine; Mao rebelled against all regularity. Mao read voraciously. Jiang Qing was too impatient to read. Mao prided himself on his health and physical prowess; Jiang Qing wallowed in her illnesses. They would not even eat the same food. Mao relished his hot and spicy Hunan dishes while Jiang Qing insisted on either blandly cooked fish and vegetables or fancied herself a connoisseur of the "Western" food she had eaten in the Soviet Union—pot roast and caviar.[15] She had never learned to swim and was embarrassed that her right foot had six toes. She kept her feet covered with rubber shoes even when she waded into the ocean.[16]

In the early years of Mao's rule she abided by the stipulation handed down by the leaders of the Party. "In the mid-1950s her words had little bite. Years later, during the Cultural Revolution, her vicious indictments would destroy careers and lives."[17] She didn't become more outspoken on political issues until 1963. She used her artistic background to intertwine traditional Chinese art forms[18] with proletarian themes. This eventually led to the disastrous Cultural Revolution.

Her and her associates' loyalty to Mao elevated them to higher positions within the government and the party structure. Her fiery speeches to mass gatherings of the Red Guard movement and her

---

[15] Ibid., 140–41.
[16] Ibid., 175.
[17] Ibid., 143.
[18] *Encyclopedia Britannica, Inc.*

denunciation of so-called right-wing and supposedly counterrevolutionary sentiments held by some top officials surrounding Lui Shaoqui, chairman of the People's Republic of China, and Deng Xiaoping, gave her more clout. She emerged as the most influential woman of China. "Mao had every reason to trust his wife politically. Without her husband she was nothing. And Jiang Qing could at last fulfill her political ambitions."[19]

After the deaths of Zhou Enlai on January 8, 1976 and Mao Zedong on September 9, 1976, her power waned quickly. Posters plastered on walls in Beijing denouncing her and the other members of the Gang of Four finally led to their imprisonment. She was stripped of her membership in the Communist Party, tried for counterrevolutionary crimes, and received a suspended death sentence, which was commuted to life imprisonment in 1983. She committed suicide on May 14, 1991.

An Unforgettable Night

The preceding pages describe the political backdrop for another of my visits to China. Very few cars traveled the narrow, poorly lit Shanghai streets. Rain pelted pedestrians and others who scurried by on their bicycles. I struggled to find the home of a Christian leader who had just been released from many years of internment. I have forgotten his name, but I shall never forget that encounter on a cold, rainy night in Shanghai. Officials gave him a three-week furlough after which he had to return to the camp.

I entered his home, not sure what the evening would hold. We sat across from each other at a makeshift table. His wife busied herself fixing the traditional green tea. When I asked some questions, his eyes darted back and forth at first. He had never seen me before. *Can I trust him?* he must have asked himself as we studied each other.

---

[19] Li Zhisui, 408.

"How can you cope with the prospect of leaving your wife and children once more?" I asked. "You were forcefully separated from your loved ones for years, and now you have to leave them again."

He sat silently for a long time. Finally he looked up and said, "I have had the joy of baptizing several hundred new believers in the camp over the years. That is my flock, and as their shepherd I belong there."

"But you have not seen your wife and your kids in years," I objected. "You cannot leave them again."

He stared into the cup of hot tea that warmed his hands in this cold room.

"I will go back gladly," he answered. "They need me."

Grief and disbelief overcame me. This man of God had suffered so much, and I could do nothing to dissuade him. He did not possess much in worldly goods. He probably didn't own more than the flimsy jacket on his back. But he counted it all loss and looked forward to serving his people, the ones whom he had led to the Lord and who needed to be nourished in their spiritual lives.

He was the first one who exposed me to the horrific plight of Christians who had suffered so much for their faith. Others would follow.

Through Deep Waters

Wang Mingdao glanced at me through ill-fitting spectacles. "Yes, I denied my Lord, but He has forgiven me," he whispered. He could hardly talk. He was eighty-three years old on the day I saw him.

His friends had led me to his apartment building. Recognizing the area, I knew it was near the place where I had lived forty years earlier. The streets and lanes hadn't changed. We climbed the creaky stairs leading to his weatherbeaten door. The paint had blistered and peeled away from the wood. The Chinese lived in apartments that had not been cared for in decades. Their disastrous condition explained the cheap rent. All of it was government property, and no one cared for the upkeep.

I sat in rapt attention as he told me his story. I looked into the face of one of the great preachers and evangelists of his time. As a young boy I had heard about him, and now he sat across from me.

"I remember preaching in the province where your parents used to work," he continued. "Those were great days. We had the freedom to preach all over China. As a pastor in Beijing, I had many responsibilities, but I loved to travel and preach the gospel."

"What happened then?" I had heard so much about this man of God, but I wanted to hear it directly from him.

"You work with Billy Graham," he said, changing the subject. "He is a great evangelist, but I don't agree with his posture toward our government."

"What do you mean?" I asked.

Because his English was quite good, he did not need an interpreter. Sometimes he struggled for the appropriate words, but he could make himself understood. I sensed some apprehension as he continued.

"I heard that Billy Graham wants to visit me. But I am not ready to receive him. He plays along with those who hold power in our country. Those people are enemies of our Lord."

He came across as a hurt man, struggling to forgive and to forget what others had done to him.

"But Billy Graham is a man of God," I explained. "He holds evangelistic crusades all over the world and would love to do it here also. He has led thousands to the Lord. I understand this is not possible right now, but perhaps that time will come. The Chinese government has given him permission to preach in churches, however. While he is here, he would love to meet people like you."

"I don't agree with his preaching in churches under the control of the Three-Self Patriotic Movement (TSPM)." He raised his voice when he said that, adamant about his position.

Wang Mingdao had gone through deep waters. After the communists had conquered the nationalist armies and established a new China, the government asked all Christians to sign a statement denouncing imperialism and with it the work of foreign mission organizations. A new organization would unite all churches under the banner of the Three-Self Principles. These principles were not new. Missionaries, such as Henry Venn of the Church Mission Society and Rufus Anderson of the American Board of Commissioners for Foreign Missions, had popularized them in the nineteenth century. Those principles were good, sound, and logical. Churches in any given country should stand on their own feet. Self-support, self-government, and self-propagation must be the foundational principles by which all churches are run.

"But in China these Three-Self Principles are placed under the guidance of the communist party," he persisted, "and I did not agree with that. So they imprisoned my wife and me."

"I Denied My Lord"

Rev. Wang suffered in prison where his captors brainwashed him. For hours on end guards forced prisoners to write down their faults, mistakes, vices, and anything else that contradicted the governing powers. After having been scrutinized, the papers were given back to their owners to complete a more honest self-evaluation. After months of such exercises, individuals broke. In sheer desperation prisoners either agreed with their torturers or committed suicide. Many took their own lives; others confessed. Wang Mingdao broke and confessed. When he signed a statement denying his Lord, he was set free.

"I walked the streets of Beijing in disbelief. I wept again and again. I had denied my Lord," he said. "I chastised myself and sobbed, 'I am Peter, I am Peter, and I denied my Lord.'"

Both of us sat in silence. He was hard of hearing. An old-fashioned hearing aid in his right ear connected to an amplifying box on his lap via a thin gray cable. His wife looked on, wiping away tears. Both of them were so frail. Old, worn-looking things cluttered their room. Nonessentials filled a table next to a window. They had stacked study books on crude bookshelves. A hot broth simmered in a wok in the other corner. Despite being in the twilight years of their lives, both projected a dynamic spiritual faith. These saintly people encouraged me.

He picked up the thread again and raised his voice once more. "Yes, I was Peter, but I was not Judas. I never was Judas," he repeated. As we all know, Judas committed suicide, but Peter became a rock of the early church.

"What would you like to share with Christians in the western world?" I asked.

Without hesitation he quoted Revelation 2:10, "Don't be afraid of what you are about to suffer. The devil will throw some of you into prison and put you to the test. You will be persecuted for ten days. Remain faithful even when facing death and I will give you the crown of life."

My Savior Leads Me

Wang Mingdao started to sing with a quivering voice. He could not hold a tune, but it was beautiful in a different way. The song came from his heart. His wife joined him. As tears filled my eyes, I sang along too.

All the way my Savior leads me,
What have I to ask beside?
Can I doubt His tender mercy,
Who through life has been my Guide?
Heav'nly peace, divinest comfort,
Here by faith in Him to dwell!

For I know, whate'er befall me,
Jesus doeth all things well;
For I know, whate'er befall me,
Jesus doeth all things well.

Nothing could mirror his deep feelings and allegiance to his Lord better than this song. Wang Mingdao identified his sufferings with Fanny Crosby (1820–1915). Even though she became blind at only six weeks of age because of an eye infection that could not be treated during her time, she bore her infirmity with dignity and never became bitter. She enjoyed a fulfilled life, writing this hymn and hundreds of others to praise her Creator.

Wang Mingdao and Fanny Crosby knew something of what is expressed in the next two stanzas.

All the way my Savior leads me
Cheers each winding path I tread,
Gives me grace for every trial,
Feeds me with the living Bread.
Though my weary steps may falter
And my soul athirst may be,
Gushing from the Rock before me,
Lo! A spring of joy I see;
Gushing from the Rock before me,
Lo! A spring of joy I see.

All the way my Savior leads me
O the fullness of His love!
Perfect rest to me is promised
In my Father's house above.
When my spirit, clothed immortal,
Wings its flight to realms of day
This my song through endless ages:
Jesus led me all the way;
This my song through endless ages:
Jesus led me all the way.

Wang Mingdao had found his rest, even before he had gone to heaven.

An Aphorism For Christians

by Wang Mingdao

One should establish oneself on the foundation of fearing God. One should love one's neighbor as the way of life. Be absolutely honest with others. Discipline yourself strictly. When in humble and destitute circumstances, never flatter others. When in wealth and high position, never be proud.

One should never be envious. Rejoice with those who benefit and never rejoice in the calamity of others. Share sorrow with those who are under adversity.

When with others, if benefit occurs, don't rush forward for it. When working with others, if danger occurs, don't flinch. If you have offended others or broken things of others, you should admit your fault and pay the damage.

If you are offended or wronged, be lenient. If you have benefited others, consider it your duty. If others benefit you, consider it their benevolence and be grateful.

When handling money, large or small sums, be honest, clean, and upright. When making friends—male or female—be fair, frank, and pure of mind. Don't make a promise rashly; whenever it is made, work hard to fulfill it. If it is not a must, don't borrow; when borrowed, repay or return as soon as possible. Revere one's elders as well as others' elders. Love one's own children as well as others'.

Seeing other's good qualities, make them your model. Seeing other's shortcomings, make them your warning examples. Restrain yourself; be slow to anger and slow to become impatient. Guard your mouth and be slow to speak. Don't spread words when you have no evidence. Don't act unbecomingly.

Don't have absurd desire for others' wealth. Don't watch with folded arms over others' difficulties; help them when possible. Don't give flattering titles to men. Don't judge and criticize others behind their back. When working for others, be diligent and loyal. When dealing with people, be honest and frank. Detest evil things as one detests scorpions. Admire righteousness as one admires pearls. It is better to lose one's money, but don't lose trust.

It is better to give up your life than to brag on your good qualities. Have good manners and speak politely. Have a clean body and clothes. Don't do things that incur disgust; don't speak words that incur dislike. Refrain from smoking, drinking, and gambling. Abandon seductive clothing and ornament. Think of others whatever you do. Glorify God wherever you go.

—Translated from Chinese into English by an anonymous person

Chapter 5

God's Call—The Third Generation

"The elder of our church wants to send you off with a banquet," the young pastor in Nanchang told us after we had concluded our teaching assignment in his city. The Chinese typically express their thanks this way. After all, their food is good, and they like to impress their foreign guests with such culinary delights.

We met in a restaurant where a private room had been reserved for us. Dinner was served at a round table. This is a wonderful way to communicate with your friends. Everyone has a chance to listen and to be part of the conversation.

On occasions like this, the Chinese usually serve ten or more dishes. Waiters bring in particularly chosen delights one at a time. Most of them are delicious; however, on occasion you don't know what you are eating. Once when tiny turtles were offered to me to suck on, I almost passed out. How do you eat them when they're still tucked inside a protective shell? But I did. It would be an affront to the host to reject such an expensive delicacy. In impossible situations, however, I also learned to deliver indigestible "junk food" under the table without being seen.

When the elder stood to say grace, the servers did not mind. I never have seen Christians sit down for a meal in public places embarrassed or frightened to pray openly. The first time I vividly experienced this was in Fuzhou. Our host had reserved three large round tables in an open restaurant and had invited functionaries of the Religious Affairs Bureau.[20] They are communists and atheists. The host stood and said grace with a loud voice so that all participants of our party could hear him. When the Chinese pray, they pray long prayers. Hearing him overpower the chatter of all the others sitting in that restaurant amazed me. Where else would you see such boldness? We try to mask our prayers by scratching our foreheads. At least I have done that. But here, surrounded by communists, Christians stand up for what they believe and testify to those who otherwise may never hear about Jesus Christ.

Generations Mean A Lot

Before our dinner in Nanchang, the elder made a little speech. He was over eighty years old. One lonely tooth protruded from the right side of his mouth. Looking at me he said, "You and I are old." Under my breath I said, "Thanks." He continued, "Thank you for coming to Nanchang to help us. Many years ago, before the liberation, your parents served in this province. But you have not forgotten us. You came back to carry on where your folks had to leave off. Thank you."

And then he turned to my son Erik. "Your grandparents represented the first generation of your family to come to China. Your dad represents the second. And you stand for the third generation. Thank you for coming."

The Chinese think in generations. When you have a four to five thousand year history, generations mean a lot.

The Chinese don't appreciate short endeavors. The longer the better. Three generations make a strong statement. You believe in

[20] The name of this government department was later changed to the State Administration of Religious Affairs (SARA). To avoid confusion, I will continue to use the old term.

what you are doing, and you are willing to stick it out. Even though your parents were forced out, you did not mind. You came back. We deeply appreciate that. We value your resolve. Please continue what you are doing.

But he was not through. With a shaky voice he continued, "Your father and I are old." With that he reached over and grabbed Erik's hand, pulled it across the table, and then reached out for the hands of two young pastors. In midair he brought them together, saying, "You from the West, and they from the East, join together to spread the gospel in our land. Thank you."

The elder's gesture deeply moved Erik and touched me as well. After eleven years with Youth for Christ, Erik had joined me in the China ministry. He knew it was an important task, but until then he never had felt a distinct call to China. He had shared this with me in earlier conversations.

"I wanted to work with my father," he said. "Then I realized the phenomenal opportunity to serve Christ, representing the third generation of our family in China."

He had always known that he was serving his Lord. He loved his work. He loved the Chinese, and he loved serving the Chinese church. But at that moment Erik knew that God had placed him at the right spot. By continuing what his grandparents had been forced to leave, Erik found himself in the center of God's will for his life.

A third generation of missionary involvement was born.

Little did I know this incident would strengthen the hands of our other son who, like his grandparents before him, worked the fields faithfully but did not see fruit right away.

Encouragement Beyond China

Berlin, Germany is far away from Nanchang. Thousands of the government's elite of the German Democratic Republic (GDR) lived in Marzahn, one of the many suburbs, where our second son Heiko and his family set up a home in 1995 to work as missionaries. The Communist Party enjoyed a stronghold in Marzahn. Its citizens still vote mostly for the new party (PDS—party of the Socialists) that was formed to take the place of the former Communist Party after the demise of the GDR. When planners laid out the city with its *Plattenbauten,*[21] they omitted churches from the drawing board—an indication of the nation's spiritual vacuum. These ugly looking living quarters, which were given to the faithful of the party, became the envy of all citizens. Thousands of families from across East Germany had moved there to show off the party's achievements.

But everything changed after the fall of the Berlin wall. Like in China, doors opened slowly to those who wanted to bring Christ to a materialistic and atheistic society. But it was tough going. After two years of faithful ministry, our son saw no fruit. Heiko became discouraged and depressed. Inge and I traveled to Berlin to bring him some comfort. "Remember your grandparents," I said. "They stayed twenty-five years in spite of the terrible odds they faced and did not retreat in the light of seeming failure. Faithfulness is what counts and not success as seen with the world's eyes."

Then I told him of the encounter I had with the young pastor in Nanchang who thanked God for missionaries who had given their lives to missions in China. Fifty years had to pass to reveal the phenomenal impact missionaries have had on building Christ's kingdom in China. From that moment on Heiko never looked back.

Like my parents and my son Heiko, I needed to trust God when my desire to advance His kingdom met with some unforeseen obstacles. My passion for training Chinese evangelists quickly became an exercise in waiting for God's timing.

---

[21] Huge blocks of apartment buildings constructed mainly with ugly slabs of concrete.

Chapter 6

Delayed But Not Deterred

I had fallen into a deep sleep. The Apollo Hotel, situated next to a small yet beautiful lake in downtown Amsterdam, had been my home for many months. At eleven o'clock at night the telephone rang and jarred me awake. I instantly recognized Billy Graham's voice on the other end. It was five o'clock in the afternoon his time.

"How are you doing?" he asked. "I hope I did not disturb you." I never felt disturbed when he called, no matter how late it was. Even though I wished his timing had been better that night, I acted like I was wide awake.

"Werner, we need to go to plan B. We may have to phase out the preparations for the conference. We don't have the money yet to continue, and I will never go into debt. I never have. And I will not now."

His call stunned me. For months we had been preparing for the largest evangelists' conference ever held up to that time.[22] He wanted to invite 5,000 evangelists from around the world to be trained, challenged, and blessed in matters that were close to his heart: world evangelization (Amsterdam '83). And now this. Before asking me to direct the

[22] The second conference for itinerant evangelists was held in 1986, also directed by the author. The third such conference was held in 2000. All of them were in Amsterdam.

International Conference for Itinerant Evangelists (ICIE), he had made it very clear that he would go through with his vision only if the money for this large undertaking was in the bank. When asked who was responsible for fundraising, he said, "I am."

On another occasion he and I had strolled through the Vondelpark in downtown Amsterdam, located near the Apollo Hotel. He showed me how to walk properly to enhance the cardiovascular system of our bodies. He swung his arms forcefully as he stepped up his pace. I knew that he had been an ardent jogger, but in his later years he preferred walking. "After the age of forty you should stop jogging. It is bad for your knees," he advised me.

At that time he shared his dream to extend his passion for evangelistic preaching to itinerant evangelists serving in even the remotest corners of the world. I knew it would be a monumental task to bring this about. I thought of China. What about the evangelists in a tightly controlled country like China?

A few weeks after this call, he called again and gave me the green light to go back to plan A. So we were on the roll again. I visited China with twenty open airline tickets for Chinese evangelists to attend this conference. While visiting with Bishop Ting,[23] who at that time was the President of the China Christian Council, I showed him those tickets. All that was needed was to select the evangelists, put their names on those tickets, and send them to Amsterdam. But we faced one obstacle.

Frustrated By Flags

We had planned to have a parade of flags during the opening ceremonies of the conference. A great idea! As long as the Kuomintang flag from Taiwan would be displayed on the same platform, however,

---

[23] I decided to spell his name the way he spells it in his personal letters to me: Ting. Others opted for Ding.

this would not work for China. In fact, this flag display kept Chinese evangelists from attending the conference.

I argued against flags, but I was overruled. In heaven we won't have flags, I reasoned. But I could not convince the others. Flags had to be displayed to add credence to an international conference. So we did not have anyone present from the most populous country of the world.

This turn of events disappointed me since China was experiencing the fastest church growth of any country in the world. I desperately wanted Chinese evangelists to rub shoulders with their counterparts with whom they had not had any contact so far. I wanted them to receive the same kind of teaching. I also wanted them to experience the bond that unites all Christians from around the world, no matter what their race, nationality, or denomination. But the insistence on displaying flags resulted in the misfortune of not having participants from China.

So the largest country of the world was not represented. Discussing this with Billy Graham after the conference, I suggested taking much of the teaching done at Amsterdam to China. If Chinese evangelists can't leave their country, why don't we find a way to engage them in their home country? He agreed.

Another Setback

On several trips to China I offered this kind of training to the church leadership. I was always reminded of the Three-Self Principles, which the registered church had adopted. Staying true to my principles never to do anything illegally, I waited for a more opportune time. That time came in 1988 when Bishop Ting finally said, "Let's try it, let's do it." But then the June 4, 1989 incident on Tiananmen Square in Beijing brought everything to a screeching halt.

Young Chinese students clamored for more democracy, and a movement was born. Multitudes of students, later joined by young factory workers and others, assembled on the Tiananmen Square in Beijing. Day after day of peaceful manifestations turned into long weeks. A twenty-seven-foot-tall statue, similar to the Statue of Liberty in New York, was erected and cheered on by tens of thousands of frustrated yet determined young people. They called it the "goddess of democracy." They came from all over China as their parents had done some twenty years earlier during the height of the Cultural Revolution, which began in 1966 and lasted ten years.

At that time, hundreds of thousands of young people had raised their voices while waving their "red bibles."[24] They laughed, wept, sang, and shouted while paying homage to their great leader Mao Zedong. I still remember watching those frightful scenes on television. They gathered in trance-like ecstasy, screaming at the top of their voices like the misled youth of Nazi Germany. How fearsome when masses are swept away in total allegiance to a human being! What awful legacies Hitler and Mao have left behind!

But this was different. Disillusioned young people wanted more freedom. A number of them had traveled overseas and seen a vibrant democracy bring about a society that honored human rights and true liberty. With it a pulsating economy emerged, and this appealed to most young Chinese observers.

But democracy in its true form must be understood and then developed and experienced properly, otherwise it will be misused. Political and national leaders only gradually accepted democracy in its infancy under the Athenian (Greek) statesman Pereclisis (495–429 BC). It took centuries to improve. Each country had to find its own way. Even today world leaders interpret democracy differently. China has a long history of dynasties where democratic thinking was not readily espoused. In Europe the French revolution had rallied around

---

[24] "The first edition of the 'Quotations from Chairman Mao' was published in May 1964. It was a small book. No bigger than the palm of a hand, covered in gaudy red plastic and filled with aphorisms drawn from Mao's speeches and writings." Li Zhisui, *The Private Life of Chairman Mao* (New York: Random House, 1994), 412.

the slogan *"Liberté, Egalité, Fraternité."* Hundreds of years before this, the Scots fought for independence from England, as depicted in the film *Brave Heart*. The Americans did the same in the eighteenth century, when Patrick Henry declared from the pulpit of St. John's church in Richmond, Virginia, "Give me liberty or give me death."

Even the United States had to learn democracy. The civil rights movement of the 1960s and 1970s showed the nation's struggle toward equality for all races. Battles raged across the country, especially at college campuses. The Kent State University riots turned deadly. Tempers erupted and blood was spilled to achieve human rights. And this happened in the latter part of the twentieth century! I was rudely made aware of this when China's Premier Wen Jiabao gave a speech at Harvard University entitled "Turning Your Eyes to China."

He zeroed in on human rights issues.

> I am not suggesting that China's human rights situation is impeccable. . . . In China it would be a time-consuming process to develop China's democracy perfectly. But as you look at the U.S. history it is also time-consuming for [the] U.S. to develop its democracy from the days of the Declaration of Independence in the year 1776 to the Civil War in the 1860s, and to the incidents of Martin Luther King in the 1960s.

Without excusing the human rights infringements, we must see these issues in the greater context of history. John Fraser writes in his book *The Chinese:*

> Many Chinese, grown accustomed to the reality around them, would not acknowledge many of the things we in the West consider human-rights abuses. Part of the reason for this is caught up in history. Chinese governments have traditionally sought to leave a strong imprint on the people's consciousness. To survive as a nation with such a huge population has necessitated a degree of cohesiveness in society that can be traced back

> thousands of years to the first efforts at controlling flooding along the bank of the Yellow River, the heartland of Chinese civilization. The Chinese Communist Party is the inheritor of an ancient propensity for ordering human affairs in an extremely rigid and doctrinaire fashion.[25]

After the tanks had rolled over barricades and fired into the crowds, I immediately traveled to Beijing. Wanting to see firsthand what had happened, I stepped out of my taxi and walked toward the Mao mausoleum. A police officer waved me back into my taxi. As the driver circled around the Tiananmen Square (Heavenly Square), I saw marks of scorched cement. When I asked the driver what really had happened, he shrugged his shoulders. He seemed frightened to speak.

Much had happened on that fateful day. A movement with a noble cause had been crushed. It is futile to argue who was right and who was wrong. The young people wanted to bring about a peaceful change, but the government felt obliged to step in when challenged. Only history will reveal the true story.

Bishop Ting's Appeal

"Now we have to wait before pursuing the plans for you to bring in a teaching team," Bishop Ting told me after that episode. He had been critical of the government's handling of the situation. Some students of the theological seminaries in Beijing and Nanjing had marched with the demonstrators, and others had supplied them with food and drinks.

During the events leading up to the Beijing massacre, as western journalists quickly labeled the confrontation on June 4, 1989, the bishop made the following appeal:

---

[25] John Fraser, *The Chinese* (New York: Summit Books, 1980), 391.

On May 18, I issued the following statement as president of the China Christian Council and Chair of the Christian Three-Self Patriotic Movement Committee:

> We wholeheartedly affirm the student demonstrations in Beijing, Shanghai, and other cities in recent days. The hunger strikes are a patriotic activity. Their demands arise from a feeling of patriotism.
>
> We sincerely hope and call upon the top-level leaders of the Central Committee of the Chinese Communist Party and the State Council to carry on a dialogue with the students as soon as possible.
>
> We deeply hope that the students end their hunger strikes and take care of their health. Our motherland needs you.

I wish to add that I am glad that Christians are making their presence felt in these demonstrations. I am very glad that the students in the Nanjing Theological Seminary are taking an active part. They not only join the demonstrations but also try to serve their fellow students by sending them drinking water and bread. I understand that Christians in Beijing are also playing an active role.

I have joined with some forty other members of the Standing Committee of the National People's Congress to propose that there should be an emergency meeting of the Standing Committee to be called as soon as possible to discuss the whole question so that the democratic process could be facilitated and bloodshed avoided.

We are grateful for the patriotic action of the people of Hong Kong in supporting our motherland, and we ask that Christians around the world continue to remember us in their prayers.

Bishop K. H. Ting
May 23, 1989

The bishop, who is a great patriot, was asked to explain his position. I was told that he believed two issues needed to be dealt with: freedom or democracy, and the massive corruption that had permeated the political leadership in China. He thwarted the critics by focusing on the corruption within the communist party that had an immense negative influence on the population and was therefore unhealthy for the country. The officials agreed with his assessment. His stand toward the immediate issue at hand, however, which had motivated so many students, intellectuals, and even common workers to clamor for more democracy was gently yet thoroughly swept under the carpet.

Gotthard Oblau, a German theologian who had lived in China for ten years, made some interesting remarks in an article written in 2001.

> It was also Bishop Ting more than any other church leader who hoped that church congregations would, over time, prove themselves to be laboratories and schools for democracy. It was Ting's hope that congregations ordering their finances and other affairs in an independent and democratic way, and calling people to participation and also accountability, would show themselves to be cells of a future civil society within a Chinese society which has traditionally been structured in a very hierarchical fashion and in which all blessings are expected from the state. Ting talked of such visions most frequently in the period after the defeat of the democracy movement of 1989, a time when cynicism and political despondency spread rapidly throughout China.
>
> The bishop's students in the seminary respected and loved him for his stance. Even though he was approaching eighty, they used to say that he was at least a generation younger at heart.[26]

---

[26] Gotthard Oblau, "*Theology Needs Freedom. Personal notes on a questionable campaign within China's church.*"

Desire Fulfilled

Two years went by. In the spring of 1991, the first China Partner team spent ten days lecturing at the Nanjing Theological Seminary. Team members came from Germany, Jamaica, New Zealand, and the United States. Before arriving in Nanjing, I had wanted to travel once more through the province of Jiangxi where my parents had worked for so many years. The time had come for me to step into their footsteps. Our eldest son Erik had come along. He represented the third generation of our family working in China. From the capital city of Nanchang we took the train north to Jiu Jiang. My parents had often traveled through Jiu Jang on their way from Shanghai to their mission station.

This was a nostalgic trip for me. In Jiu Jiang we boarded the river steamer for Nanjing. The foggy weather prompted our crew to blast a horn every thirty seconds to warn other vessels of possible danger. As evening fell, I went on deck and listened to the propellers as they labored against the muddy waters, turning them into churning white bubbles that disappeared into the ever-darkening distance. I reminisced about my parents who had stood on steamers like this one and looked into muddy waters. I thanked God for such a heritage. My eyes moistened as I remembered the hardships they had encountered in a strange yet beloved land.

Now it was my time to pick up the torch and carry on what they had started but were forced to abandon in 1950. I vowed to stay faithful to such a sacred calling. I stood at the threshold of an exciting ministry. The following day this steamer, now struggling through the fog, would arrive at the city that would make or break what I had set out to do.

In 1991, Nanjing had only one skyscraper, the Jingling Hotel. You could see the massive white tower while floating down the river miles away. For ten days it was our home.

The day before beginning our lectures, I had assembled our teaching team for a briefing session. None of them had ever visited China, and they had many questions. I introduced them to Chinese history and why thousands of missionaries had come from many countries to establish a beachhead for Christ. Emotion overcame me as I shared with them the frustrations and disappointments my parents had endured. "Less than what you can count on two hands found Christ through our ministry in the twenty-five years of our stay in China," my father had told me. Being forced to leave devastated him. So many years yet so little fruit.

Despite the circumstances, God's promises are still true. "In due season we shall reap, if we faint not" (Gal. 6:9, KJV). Perhaps this would be a season of God's favor on our ministry. As our team prayed in the conference room in the Jingling Hotel in Nanjing following my remarks, I sensed the presence of the Lord. We were ready for the task ahead.

Students from across China sat in rapt attention as our team imparted biblical truths to them. Bishop Ting invited our team to a farewell banquet after we completed ten days of intense teaching. He thanked us for coming, saying, "I have not heard one negative word about what you taught or did. Please come back and teach wherever you find an open door." God had answered my prayers.

Chapter 7

What About Persecution?

It is easier to make certain things legal than to make them legitimate.

—Chamfort

As long as you live in France you must naturally submit yourself to French law." Monsieur de Villefort spoke these words, addressing the Count of Monte Cristo in Alexandre Dumas' bestselling book with the same title.[27] This expresses exactly how the Chinese see it. If anyone wants to work or minister in China, it must be done by submitting to the law of the land. This is precisely what many foreigners are *not* willing to do. Therefore China looms as a threatening monster to them.

The Need For Credible Reporting

"Everything you hear about China is true," wannabe China experts often say. In reality, those who don't know much about China use such a statement as a smoke screen to cover their lack of knowledge

[27] Alexandre Dumas, *The Count of Monte Cristo* (New York: Bantam Books, 1956), 177.

regarding China, or to explain things in such a way that those in the dark are not adequately informed. Usually they have an agenda that they want to pass on to others. Scripture admonishes us, "Any story sounds true until someone sets the record straight."[28] China is huge and thus the reporting on events difficult. Therefore, throughout the past few years, many confusing and even contradictory reports have been made about the church in China, so that people—most of them living in the western world—have become totally frustrated at best and cynical at worst. Let me give just one recent example.

"The Chinese take an incredible risk when they come to Christ. They say 'yes' to Jesus at the same time they say 'yes' to death. It's almost as if they agree, 'I will die, but I want to be a Christian.'" The CEO of a major evangelical mission organization voiced this. The news media picked it up and broadcasted his comments. This is not only a mistaken view or perception but totally wrong. But why do otherwise responsible men make such unreasonable statements? Does it help to raise more money, as someone once remarked?

Much has been written about persecution in China. Some of it was correct, but much of it was not. The above statement was not only inaccurate in some way but totally false. Therefore we must ask, "How seriously do we take the reporting on persecution?"

In order to stay credible we have to be engaged in fair, balanced, and correct reporting. If this is not done, then we have to ask what can we believe, and how seriously can we take the media? This is exactly what a young lady once asked me. The elite secular media often lacks unbiased and correct reporting, so we thank God for Christians and the Christian media for at least trying to be honest in their reporting. The above quote is false, however, and does not reflect what God is doing in China. Sadly, evangelical media outlets reported it. Facts need to be reported. Poorly researched stories, which often turn out to be false, need to be scrutinized before reaching publication or the airwaves.

---

[28] Proverbs 18:17, NLT.

Let me give you another example. The *Philadelphia Inquirer* reported the following:

> Fu and Li also have sent Bush [on the eve of the President's visit to China] a list of 123 imprisoned Christian leaders. Among them is Pastor Gong Shengliang, one of the five church leaders whose relatives Fu called this week. Gong is an evangelical Christian and founder of the South China Church, now branded a cult by Chinese police.
>
> In a document dated August 9, 2001, which was translated by Fu, the Beijing security police called for "the complete smash" of Gong's group. A Chinese court sentenced Gong to death for running a cult and for criminal offenses including arson, beatings, and rape. His niece Li Ying, thirty-six, editor of the church group magazine, received the death penalty with a two-year reprieve.
>
> Such sentences are usually commuted to life in prison. Fu said the criminal charges were bogus. He released testimony from women who said police tortured them to obtain false allegations of rape. Fu said that rather than a cult Gong practiced a brand of Christianity that would be familiar to Christians here. "They are mainstream evangelicals and should be regarded as following the faith of Billy Graham," Fu said.[29]

The evangelical media picked up this story and broadcasted it across the world. This report, if true, rightfully enraged Christians everywhere. This was another proof of persecution experienced by those who lived out their Christian faith in a suppressed society, they reasoned.

But what really happened? I don't claim that persecution has never taken place, but we need to be careful to frame such reports in the right context of what actually happened. Listen to what Danny Yu, President of Christian Leadership Exchange, wrote about this case:

---

[29] *Philadelphia Inquirer*, February 20, 2002.

> During my visit to China last month, I was talking to some friends about the South China Church. I was somewhat surprised when I was shown some photographs, which are apparently now accessible to a limited public in China but have not made their way to the West yet. There are photographs of Mr. Gong Shengliang with his female followers.
>
> The texts beneath the two pictures are identical and written in poetic form. Apparently the Chinese poem is a pledge, and the photo is taken in commemoration of the initiation or commitment ceremony. The text can be roughly translated as follows: "My Lover Teacher, I am willing to pledge: Commitment for a Lifetime (Intimacy), Togetherness in Life and in Death (Absorption), Maid Servant to be Honored through Husband (Humiliation), Rising and Falling with the Teacher (Company)."[30]

This supposedly evangelical leader distorted and misused Christianity by gathering around him a harem of duped and hoodwinked women who were humiliated, dishonored, and on occasions raped. In China the death penalty is meted out to rapists.

Let me give you another example of unsubstantiated and false statements. "In spite of intense persecution, it is estimated that 20,000 people a day receive Christ as their Savior in China." An evangelical mission organization wrote this in an evangelical magazine. Two false statements are being made here. First, there is no intense persecution of Christians for their faith going on in China these days. Second, who has counted the 20,000? These figures don't support the facts. Such unproven declarations mislead people.

And then listen to this statement. It is comical to the point of being hilarious. At a conference China Partner held recently, one of the speakers declared, "Some 30,000 people per day are coming to Christ through one mission organization alone." Then he identified that organization. This overseas organization has claimed

[30] Danny Yu, "*South China Church: A Case Study on How We Can Better Help Religious Development in China*," August 19, 2003.

such figures for the past five years! Imagine, if true, this means that one organization alone has led 55 million people to Christ! Many dispute that there are that many Christians in China today! But even if that is true, what about all of the other organizations from overseas let alone the 50,000 Chinese churches? Have they not also done something for the cause of Christ? How many came to know the Lord through them? I had to stand up and challenge such irresponsible statements. He quickly backed down when I made him aware of the above numbers.

He excused himself by saying, "I am only reporting what I heard while attending a Christian conference in Singapore."

Religious Freedom Exists

As in the above instances, the reporting of untruths does not advance the cause of Christ. It is simply wrong to spread unsubstantiated stories. To spread horror stories about people facing death once they become believers in Jesus Christ is inexcusable. Millions of Christians have said yes to Jesus without having to say yes to death. And thousands are joining this vast crowd every month. Three hundred, five hundred, and even up to 1,500 baptisms per year in any given church are not uncommon.

Recently the mission organization Evergreen reported that in the city of Yangqu over the past five years one church recorded 5,000 baptisms—that is 1,000 per year. One of the churches in Shenyang experienced close to 2,000 baptisms in 2003. Many years ago this was different, but now the Chinese can practice religion as long as they stay within the laws of the land. No one is threatened with death by having religious beliefs.

On my seventy-five plus trips to China I have yet to find one Christian who has been threatened with death on the mere grounds of following Jesus. Christians had to fear for their lives at times in the past. During the Taiping Rebellion (1850–64) a host of Christians were murdered. Over 100 missionaries and tens of thousands of native Christians were massacred during the Boxer Rebellion (1896–1901). During the early communist regime, and then again during the dark days of the Cultural Revolution, Christians were hunted and had to go underground. Many of them lost their lives, and thousands were sent to the countryside to perform hard labor. Why? Because of their faith in Christ.

Today it is different. As long as the rules, regulations, and laws of the land are respected, no one needs to fear death because of his or her faith.

No wonder Christians in the West tell me that they are confused about what they hear in regard to China. We constantly have to rectify the wrong perception they receive from certain individuals. Again, let us be honest and continue to report only well-researched facts. Bad news sells better than good news. But as Christians we need to set an example in honesty and integrity. Once substantiated facts have been released, let the chips fall where they may.

Mark Galli, in a *Christianity Today* article, "The Chinese Church's Delicate Dance," gives us his opinion about persecution in China:

> And yet Christians, along with many other religionists, get arrested regularly and are often treated brutally in prison. Is this harassment of Christians as such? Not necessarily. The fact is, the government goes after anyone who for any reason reports on Chinese prison torture. Would it be better to simply call it severe human-rights abuse? Maybe, but some Communist officials still harbor deep animosity toward this Western "imperialist" religion and make up excuses to go after believers, especially if they have contacts with the West. Of course, for those languishing in prison unjustly, it's mere semantics whether it's "Christian persecution" or general "human-rights abuse."[31]

---

[31] Mark Galli, "The Chinese Church's Delicate Dance," *Christianity Today*, November 2004.

For most well-informed believers in China, it is not persecution but prosecution that Christians may experience. The state prosecutes people, including Christians, for breaking the laws of the land. They do not prosecute them for being followers of Jesus Christ. As to brutalities meted out to prisoners, whether Christian or non-Christian, those are human-rights issues. They should be dealt with as such.

Availability Of Bibles

Just yesterday an attractive young lady greeted me in the St. Andrews Presbyterian Church in Newport Beach, California. "I was so blessed to hear about what you are doing in China," she said. "My husband and I are supporting a ministry that is smuggling Bibles into China. How can you work freely in a land where persecution is the order of the day?"

"Today more than two million Bibles are printed in China every year," I informed her. In 2003, 4.17 million Bibles and New Testaments came off the press. And in 2004, 5.43 million of them were printed.

"Why then do they keep smuggling Bibles?" she pondered.

I am glad for every Bible that finds its way into China, but it is so much more expedient, efficient, and cheaper to buy them in China and distribute them there. Over 42 million Bibles and New Testaments (January 2005 statistics) have been printed in China since the Cultural Revolution. They even export them—legally. In 2003, 1.31 million Bibles were printed for other countries.

Listen to what Elder Ji Jianhong, Chairman of the TSPM, whose father was originally a Presbyterian evangelist but later became a coworker of Ni Tuosheng (Watchman Nee), told me. Ji, already in 1982, shortly after the Cultural Revolution, had persuaded the authorities to have 450,000 Bibles printed by the printing press of the People's Liberation Army (PLA). This same printing press had published *Selected Thoughts of Chairman Mao*. The world got to know it as the "red bible."

Besides those printed at the printing press of the PLA, another two million came off other secular printing presses. More than 40 million[32] were printed at the Amity Printing Company, Ltd., (APC) located in the outskirts of Nanjing, the capital city of the province Jiangsu. This printing press was founded in 1988 and built with the help of western Bible societies.

God's Work In China

One week after having heard the above false statement about the ones facing death when saying yes to Jesus, I was back in China. Firecrackers were going off—firecrackers of joy. The sun shone brightly. Hundreds of Christians had assembled on the grounds of the new Jiangxi Provincial Bible School in the provincial capital of Jiangxi. Red balloons, red lanterns,[33] and even a mammoth, blown-up red plastic arch hung in the sky. A huge red cross stood on top of one of the two new buildings. It looked beautiful against the backdrop of a lucent blue sky. Everything seemed to be in red—the color of joy in China. It had rained the day before, but "today the Lord is smiling down on this historic event," Lin Feng, president of the school, said.

Our Chinese brethren dedicated the first two buildings of the new Jiangxi Bible School. What a privilege to share in their celebration.

In 1992, the phone rang in my Florida condo. Lin Feng was on the other end, making a long distance call from Nanchang, China. He had been a student at the Jingling Theological Seminary in Nanjing,

---

[32] In the first eleven months of 2004, 4,894,000 Bibles and New Testaments were printed—the highest amount in one year since the founding of Amity. (Source: Amity Printing Company.)

[33] The history of the Chinese red lanterns can be traced back more than 2,000 years to the Western Han Dynasty (206 BC–AD 24). Then people were hanging red lanterns at their gates to celebrate the Lantern Festival, which falls on the fifteenth day of the first Chinese lunar month.

the capital city of the province Jiangsu, when our team had given a series of lectures over a period of ten days. Now he was back in his hometown. "Can you come over and help us?" he asked. "We want to start a Bible school in my city. It will be the first one in our province." My parents had labored without much fruit in this same province.

Soon after the call, one of our China Partner teams faced eighteen students on the balcony of a dilapidated church. They had come from the countryside of one of the most impoverished provinces of China. These emerging young Christian leaders focused their attention on us foreigners. What a fascinating experience to look into their hungry eyes. In no other country have I seen students take such copious notes. They had come to learn, and they wanted to learn fast. Determined to absorb as much as they could, they looked forward to disseminating the newly learned truths to their friends back home. It was a joy to teach.

Those students overcame some daunting circumstances—crude desks, no blackboard, appalling living quarters, and hygienic facilities impossible to describe. But they had come to learn how best to serve their Master.

They did not have any professional teachers. A handful of pastors and some laypersons tried their best to teach. One of them, already over eighty years old, had weathered the Cultural Revolution. For many years he had been forced to live in the backcountry. He was one of many who had been persecuted for his faith. It was hard labor for him. But he had remained true to His Lord. Now he was back to lead the small remaining flock.

He and his fellow citizens, most of them non-Christians, had gone through one of the most traumatic episodes China has ever experienced. The Chinese were shell-shocked. Some of their friends and family members were among the millions who had been beaten, tortured, and executed. Their spirits had been demoralized.

But the Christians seemed to fare much better. Even though they had endured the same horrific experiences, they remained calm and confident. Their trust had been in the Lord God Almighty. The wounded, disheartened non-Christians looked up to those indestructible, bold, strong, devoted, and caring Christians. They were Chinese as well—fellow citizens, but they were different. They exuded fortitude and a confidence that others lacked.

Nien Cheng was a perfect example of this. In her fascinating and revealing book she spoke of this fortitude:

> Throughout the years of my imprisonment, I had turned to God often and felt His presence. In the drab surroundings of the gray cell, I had known magic moments of transcendence that I had not experienced in the ease and comfort of my normal life. My belief in the ultimate triumph of truth and goodness had been restored, and I had renewed courage to fight on. My faith had sustained me in these the darkest hours of my life and brought me safely through privation, sickness, and torture. At the same time, my suffering had strengthened my faith and made me realize that God was always there. It was up to me to come to Him.
>
> Under the watchful eyes of the guards, I could not pray openly in the daytime. The only way I could be certain of being left alone with my prayers was to bend my head over a volume of Mao Zedong's books while I prayed to God from my tormented heart.[34]

For centuries Christians had faced persecution heroically, not only in China but also in other countries around the world. Dietrich Bonhoeffer, born in 1906 into a respected family in Breslau, Germany (now Wroclaw, Poland), became a pastor and conspired against the ruthless Nazi regime.

In his best-known book *The Cost of Discipleship,* he also talked about martyrdom, which so many Chinese Christians had experienced.

> Discipleship means allegiance to the suffering Christ, and it is therefore not at all surprising that Christians should be called upon

---

[34] Nien, *Life and Death in Shanghai,* 346–47.

> to suffer. In fact it is a joy and a token of His grace. The acts of the early Christian martyrs are full of evidence, which shows how Christ transfigures for His own the hour of their mortal agony by granting them the unspeakable assurance of His presence. In the hour of the cruelest torture they bear for His sake, they are made partakers in the perfect joy and bliss of fellowship with Him. To bear the cross proves to be the only way of triumph over suffering. This is true for all who follow Christ, because it was true for Him. To go one's way under the sign of the cross is not misery and desperation, but peace and refreshment for the soul, it is the highest joy.[35]

A few days before the war ended, Bonhoeffer was hanged. He died bravely and in peace. Barefooted he stepped to the gallows and knelt to pray before he met his Savior.

This same peace and refreshment for the soul had sustained Chinese Christians during the Cultural Revolution. The highest joy of a follower of Christ had amazed many nonbelievers.

Danny Yu, born in Hong Kong but now a US citizen living in the United States, has this to say:

> Sociologists have claimed that the ten-year period of China's Cultural Revolution was the most devastating and disastrous social engineering experiment in human history. It has been estimated that every Chinese family, without exception, was adversely affected by this "revolution." Most families lost a loved one during this time period.
>
> Religion was one of the most adversely affected areas of society. In Hong Kong, all we heard was that Christians were hauled in truckloads to labor camps and accusation meetings; the entire church in China was practically shut down, and Christianity was totally destroyed.[36]

---

[35] Dietrich Bonhoeffer, *The Cost of Discipleship* (New York: The Macmillan Company, 1995), reprinted by arrangement with Scribner, a division of Simon & Schuster, Inc. New York.

[36] Yu, "South China Church."

Throughout the centuries before, Christians in China were considered to be strangers in their own homeland. They had been influenced and led astray by foreigners, the Chinese declared. Christianity was a foreign religion, so to the Chinese, Christians were nobodies. "One more Christian is one less Chinese," they said. But now things had changed because of those faithful Chinese Christians. When churches reopened, many of those nonbelievers flocked to the worship services. They wanted to know what made Christians so different. They followed Jesus, "but who is He?" they asked. What makes Him so attractive? If He can give peace of mind and remedy to despair, and fortitude in times of total devastation and persecution, let's have Him.

One by one they started to believe. One by one they started to follow Jesus. First a few, then hundreds, and finally thousands swelled the ranks of Christian believers. Millions upon millions have found the Savior following the Cultural Revolution and joined churches. Confiscated church buildings were returned to the rightful owners in order to accommodate the crowds. The government paid back rent so that ramshackle edifices could be renovated and new ones built.

A Church Reopens

"Holy, holy, holy!" rang out in the Muen Church in Shanghai, situated next to the Peoples Square, formerly the Race Course. On September 4, 1979, hundreds of Christians had streamed to the church that early Sunday morning. It was still dark. The first ones had arrived at 5:00 A.M. The pastor had privately announced that the church would reopen. The news spread by word of mouth. No one knew how many Christians remained after the disastrous Cultural Revolution. All churches, temples, and mosques had been forcefully closed.

During that horrendous time religion was out, and atheism propagated by Marxists and Maoists was in. Bands of young people had roamed the streets and ransacked homes to eliminate believers. Vilification was the order of the day. Whoever stood in the way was cast aside. But now things started to change. Deng Xiaoping, the great survivor and compatriot of Mao Zedong with whom he had weathered the Long March, was convinced that only an open door policy would lead China out of its political and economic morass. Capitalism was reintroduced. Deng's famous saying, "As long as she catches mice, it does not matter if the cat is black or white," is now enshrined by two huge cats, one black and the other white, on the new bridge across the Gann river in Nanchang, the capital city of the Jiangxi province. With such a policy, religious freedom had to be given back to the people as well. Former pastors were encouraged to get back to work. And work they did.

An elder of the New Grace Church explained. "When I reached the church that fateful and momentous morning, the sight of so many believers overwhelmed me. For years we had been scattered and could meet only secretly in our homes. We did not know how many had stayed true to the Lord. But amazingly, multitudes showed up. We all wanted to crowd into the church, but hours before the organist intoned the beloved hymn 'Holy, holy, holy! Lord God Almighty!' the building was jam-packed. Hundreds of us could not get in. I shall never forget the words that moved us all."

Holy, holy, holy! Lord God Almighty!
Early in the morning our song shall rise to Thee;
Holy, holy, holy, merciful and mighty!
God in three Persons, blessed Trinity!

Holy, holy, holy! All the saints adore Thee,
Casting down their golden crowns around the glassy sea;
Cherubim and seraphim falling down before Thee,
Who was, and is, and evermore shall be.

Holy, holy, holy! Though the darkness hide Thee,
Though the eye of sinful man Thy glory may not see;

Only Thou art holy; there is none beside Thee,
Perfect in power, in love, and purity.

Holy, holy, holy! Lord God Almighty!
All Thy works shall praise Thy Name in earth, and sky, and sea;
Holy, holy, holy; merciful and mighty!
God in three Persons, blessed Trinity!

"As we sang verse after verse, people started to weep," she described. "We all wept. Not one eye remained dry. It was like the days of Ezra in the Old Testament. Joy overcame us. God is still on the throne. This proved again that God is the Holy One, He is almighty, and nothing and nobody will be able to crush Him. During the bleakest days of the Cultural Revolution we knew that God would not forsake us. His staff and righteousness would lead us through the valley of death and darkness. And He did. That's why we Chinese believers love the Twenty-Third Psalm."

The first church to reopen was the *Bai Nian Tang* in Ningbo in the province of Zhejiang on April 8, 1979. Others followed in rapid succession. For a while two new churches for every three days were either reopened or newly built. By 2004, China had over 17,000 Protestant church buildings plus 30,000 registered meeting points (house churches) totaling almost 50,000 churches, not counting multitudes of unregistered groups.

The Fruit Of Their Labors

Now, some twenty years later, I stood on "God's mountain" as Li Baole calls the little hill on which the Bible school now sits. Firecrackers exploded; church leaders from Jiangxi, Hong Kong, and other Chinese cities and provinces, plus my son Erik and me, cut the ribbon. *If only my parents could be present,* I thought.

I remembered an incident after I had preached in that city a few years earlier. As usual, the church had been packed. Multitudes had stood outside listening to the sermon over loudspeakers. I saw one elderly lady on her knees praying. Others clutched their beloved Bibles. Everyone seemed to be happy.

As I made my way through throngs of people outside who had patiently endured the long service, I felt a tug on my coat. I turned to look into the face of the young pastor. Excited, he said with deep conviction, "Lin Ming Dan Muse (my name in Chinese), turn around. Look at those many, many who had to listen to your sermon outside. This is the fruit of your parents and the other missionaries who have labored here so many years ago. Praise the Lord."

Tears welled up in my eyes. I looked toward heaven where my parents are and whispered, "Thank you, Dad. Thank you, Mom, for staying faithful. I know you did not see much fruit during your twenty-five years of mission labor, and often you had been tempted to leave and go home. But you did not, because you knew that God had called you to China. In China you stayed to finish the task you were not allowed to see. Thank you. Thank you. I also say thank you on behalf of the countless Chinese Christians who now worship the living God."

Wilbur Wright (New Zealand) teaching in Nanchang in 2004

First China Partner teaching team in Nanjing 1991

Bishop K.H.Ting greeting the author in 1984

Werner and Inge Bürklin

Linchuan church dedicated in 2004

Erik and Werner Bürklin with students

Bürklin family in 1935. Author on lap of his father

Erik Burklin with Bibles printed in Nanjing

Nanchang Bible school chapel built with help of China Partner

Dedication service of Nanchang Bible school chapel

Author with Wang Mingdao shortly before Wang's death

Largest church in China (Hangzhou) dedicated in May, 2005

Bishop K.H. Ting with author in 2005

Chapter 8

The Chinese and the World

While writing this, I look out from my hotel room across the beautiful harbor of Auckland. It is hard for me to believe that this city now has over 120,000 Chinese. When the New Zealand government changed its immigration laws to open its borders further to Asian settlers, thousands from Mainland China and other Asian countries chose New Zealand as their new home. More than 50,000 young Chinese study here. Forty-eight Chinese churches in Auckland alone reach out to them.

A successful businessman whose parents had fled from the Chinese communists greeted us after we landed. Only one year old at the time of his escape, he is now in his mid-fifties. He is a prominent resident, a respected New Zealander representing the elite among his peers, and a wonderful Christian.

As I stepped into his silver-gray Mercedes Benz, he handed me a Chinese newspaper containing a full description of our ministry China Partner. Photos illustrated the work we do in the province of Jiangxi. He and Wilbur Wright, a former colleague from Youth for Christ and fellow-teacher in China from the early beginnings, had interviewed me in China after the dedication of the new Jiangxi Bible School. The next day he took me for a radio interview in Chinese to reach the Chinese community.

The enormous church growth in their former homeland apparently intrigues the Chinese. None of them had deemed this possible when they left their country for greener pastures, especially those who escaped from the new regime in the late 1940s and early 1950s.

The Chinese can now be found all over the world. In Jos, Nigeria I dined in a Chinese restaurant owned by Chinese. In Melbourne, Australia, a Chinese pastor told me about his thrilling ministry down under. A new Christian from Tianjin, a major city south of Beijing, received his PhD in the US and now operates a successful travel agency in Ft. Lauderdale, Florida. He recently joined our US board. A young pastor from northern China now serves a Chinese church in the *Ruhrgebiet*[37] in Germany. I first met him in Chengdu. China Partner helped him get his theological education at the *Neues Leben* seminary in Germany. Wherever the Chinese have gone, they have impacted society.

A Better Life?

It never has been easy for the Chinese to mix with other cultures, however. In fact, they faced much resistance and were often maligned. Instead of being welcomed in many places, they were often ostracized instead.

I more clearly understood the plight of the Chinese when I visited Arrowtown on the South Island of New Zealand. Prospectors first found gold in payable quantities in the province of Otago in 1861, and the mad rush began. Within three years this remote province had ballooned to 30,000 residents, including nearly 5,000 Chinese. Most of them had made the long and hazardous journey to that distant, isolated town from China's southern province of Guangdong. The Europeans living in the goldfields feared that these hard working Chinese would siphon off big money. To discourage more

[37] Germany's major industrial region.

immigrants from China, the government introduced a poll tax on Chinese laborers.

To alleviate some of the harshness doled out to them, the Reverend Alexander Don showed compassion on the Chinese and ministered among them from 1886–1905. He visited poor immigrants on the most remote goldfields. He spoke fluent Cantonese but made less than twenty converts. But he felt deeply for them.

What unsettled him the most? Those settlers left their homes in pursuit of a better life, as they had done in so many other countries. Initially they had wanted to stay for only a few years and then return to their homeland with their hard-earned money to buy a plot of land and live happily ever after. Only one out of seven made it back, however. The others never saw their loved ones again.

Alexander Don wrote of the plight of the Chinese in 1893:

> Here resides in Arrowtown another example of the many Chinese whose lives have been cut clean in two by emigration to the colonies. At twenty-six he married a bride of seventeen, and after only four months of wedded life, he was forced by poverty to leave home. He is now forty-nine, a confirmed opium smoker, smoking all his earnings, so there is but the faintest chance of a reunion.

Despite a history of oppression by other nations, the Chinese have overcome many obstacles. Today the Chinese enjoy increasing prosperity in their nation and around the world.

A Force In Today's World

With 1.3 billion people (the 1.3 billionth baby was born in Beijing on January 6, 2005), it is rivaled only by India, which is growing faster than China today. The landmass covers an area of about 3.6 million square miles (9.5 million square km). China covers 3,100 miles (5,000 km) from east to west and 3,400 miles (5,500 km) from north to south. Only Russia or Canada has a larger land area, and China is almost as large as Europe. Its neighbors are Mongolia, Russia, North Korea, Vietnam, Laos, Myanmar, India, Bhutan, Nepal, Pakistan, Afghanistan, Tajikistan, Kyrgyzstan, and Kazakhstan.

When I first entered China in 1981, I found it like I had left it thirty-two years earlier. Mao Zedong had liberated it from foreign domination but left it in a desperate state. Millions of its citizens (some estimate up to 50 million) had lost their lives, and the infamous Cultural Revolution had driven the Chinese into total despair. It seemed as if no hope remained for the downtrodden and the country itself. But China arose.

Just look at these amazing facts. China is not only the most populated country of the world but also boasts other records. China has:

- the longest wall in the world;
- the tallest hotel in the world, in Pudong, the eastern part of Shanghai;
- the largest construction site of the world—in Hubei;
- the largest coffer-dam of the world;
- the longest canal in the world—the Grand Canal;
- the largest city of the world—Chongqing with 31 million;
- the fastest train in the world—Transrapid built by Germany;
- the fastest growing economy in the world;
- more mobile phones than any other country in the world—over 329 million (December 2004), and 420 million expected in 2005.

Records continue to be set. In the near future China will boast:

- the largest deep water port in the world by 2009;
- the world's longest bridge, which is being built between Ningbo and Shanghai;
- 250 million cars on its roads—more than any other country.

Furthermore, the World Travel and Tourism Council predicts China will be the most visited country on the planet by 2020 and that business travel will rise by 9 percent year-by-year between 2005 and 2014.

Just think of its economic growth! It is astonishing, even stunning, considering the fact that a communist regime runs China. All other countries with communist leadership were wrecked or are bankrupt. But communists in China have become capitalists! The capitalists have taken over and are now in control.

Xinhua News Agency, China's official media outlet, reported that in the year 2002 China's annual gross domestic product exceeded 10 trillion yuan (1.21 trillion US dollars) for the first time in history, and its economic growth rate reached 8 percent. It was even better in 2003. The government announced on January 20, 2004 that China's economy grew by 9.1 percent in 2003, the fastest increase in six years. Shanghai, next to Shenzhen, is the wealthiest city on the mainland. Its economy grew by a staggering 11.8 percent. Many items are now more expensive than those in western countries. The country's economy was valued at 11.699 trillion yuan (US $1.4 trillion) in 2003. Li Deshui, the director of the National Bureau of Statistics, declared that China's gross domestic product (GDP) grew by 9.5 percent in 2004. Other major countries only dream about such achievements. And they are jealous for good reason. Sustaining economic growth is propelling China forward like no other country.

China has entered the twenty-first century with a bang. She has become one of the influential world powers. Over 20 percent of the world's population is Chinese. Since the cities of Hong Kong and Macao have reverted back under the administrative control of Beijing, China has almost achieved all of her foreign policy goals. The next plum will be Taiwan, even though this is being challenged by many inhabitants of that breakaway province. However, when the Chinese government in Beijing "codified the use of military force against Taiwan if it seeks a permanent split,"[38] close to one million Taiwanese demonstrated against the new anti-secession law. Only time will tell how those two governments will solve this delicate situation.

Over 90 percent of her population is Han Chinese, but the government woos and supports many minorities. The spoken language is as diverse as the numerous dishes on Chinese tables. Only the written language, which is the same everywhere, holds together the Chinese culture. Determined to maintain stability at all costs, a strong centralized rule from the top down enables the government to keep all factions in check. China has thirty-three administrative units directly under the central government; these consist of twenty-two provinces, five autonomous regions (such as Inner Mongolia and Tibet), four municipalities (Chongqing, Beijing, Shanghai, and Tianjin), and two special administrative regions (Hong Kong and Macao).

China is huge. The Chinese think in terms of generations, not like westerners. When asked how the French Revolution had affected the twentieth century, Chinese Premier Zhou Enlai famously replied, "It's too soon to tell."

We would love to know how China will affect the twenty-first century. My passion, however, is the Chinese church. Those Chinese living overseas are particularly suited for ministry in China.

Making An Impact For Christ

As I addressed a group of successful Kiwi Chinese Christians at a luncheon soon after my arrival in New Zealand, I could not help but see a phenomenal potential rising from Chinese just like these. What an impact they now could make in China for the cause of Christ!

"I was greatly blessed and stirred to see so many Caucasians rally around the cause of evangelism in China," a Chinese lady living in

---

[38] Associated Press, March 26, 2005.

Hong Kong told me earlier at a China symposium we sponsored in Germany. "Where are the Chinese?" she asked.

Another Chinese in Hong Kong made a similar remark. "It seems that the Caucasians have a greater burden for China than the overseas Chinese," he observed. But this is changing.

Members of the overseas Chinese community have a tremendous resource in talents, know-how, and funds! They should be at the forefront, joining with their fellow Christians in both the non-registered and registered churches. Of course, many overseas Chinese have a spiritual burden for the country of their forefathers. Quite a few of them have gone back to help, but there must be more. Yes, they are the ones who ought to go back. They know the culture. Most of them still speak Chinese, and they are sensitive to how things are being done in China. They look Chinese and blend easily.

But even here caution is needed.

Traveling in China, I often encountered resentment against those from overseas—especially those who had come with their own agenda. Unfortunately, some brilliant Chinese returned with a chip on their shoulder. They wanted to show how things could be done better, faster, cheaper, and more efficiently. They came in the same spirit of former imperialists, which did not go over well at all in today's China.

Rev. Cao Sheng-jie, the president of the China Christian Council (CCC) and a resident of Shanghai, chided the former Zhao Tian-en (Jonathan Chao) for spreading the allegation that the churches affiliated with the CCC are not interested in evangelism. She countered:

> "Evangelism has always been the task of the church. The Chinese church does care about and is involved in evangelism. But evangelism can be done in different ways. Peter through one sermon brought 3,000 people to Christ, whereas Philip led one individual from Ethiopia to Him.

"In recent years," she continues, "there are thousands who were baptized in Shanghai alone. If we don't evangelize, how do we get such results? The current status of the Chinese church is this: Whereas the quantity of believers is constantly being increased, the quality of faith is low. All kinds of superstitious teachings, heresies, and disputes have invaded our churches. For example, in one of our Shanghai churches, someone cut out his tongue to achieve a higher degree of spirituality and to avoid sin. If our goal is only to increase the numbers of believers and neglect to root out superstitions and heresies, then our churches are being built on sand and not on the Rock of Jesus Christ."[39]

These are hard and challenging words.

World Evangelization

Then there are the visionaries—the ones who dreamed about world revival at the close of the nineteenth century. John R. Mott and his associates coined the slogan "World evangelization in our generation." This laudable goal was not achieved, however.

As a young evangelist I was caught up in this fervor. I will never forget the bewilderment of the people in a German village when I pitched the Youth For Christ tent on a cow pasture. Behind the pulpit a huge banner in bold letters declared, "WORLD EVANGELIZATION IN OUR GENERATION." The tent, which seated 300, had more cows grazing outside of it than we had people inside. I meant well, and I believed in the slogan. I was convinced that I could be a part of such a grandiose achievement.

My mentor Dawson Trotman, the founder of the Navigators, taught that the world could be won to Christ in less than sixteen

---

[39] *Analysis of China Evangelization*, Shanghai Christian Council Ceremony for Fiftieth Anniversary of TSPM: Theological Thinking Construction Discussion, Special Edition.

years. As a teenager and a young convert, I heard him preach at the Free Christian Church in Shanghai, and I was spellbound. He showed us by using simple statistics that this could be done. The only hitch—every Christian had to get involved. I did not want to be left out of this phenomenal scheme. But it never happened, even with my trusting enthusiasm.

He explained, "If you lead one to Christ, then the two of you will make four, and the four of you will make eight." *Wow,* I thought. Out of eight will be sixteen and then thirty-two, sixty-four, one-hundred-twenty-eight, and on and on it goes. To follow this to its conclusion, the entire world would come to Christ within two decades. Amazing! I was stunned and excited. I wanted to be part of this God-sent chain.[40]

Betty Lee Skinner, in her book *Daws,* softened this approach by clarifying what Trotman actually meant. She writes:

> It was significant that Nav—or New Testament—principles had been defined. Producing reproducers had emerged, its survival of attacks on it confirming God's leading to preach the multiplication principle....The 2-4-8-16 idea had been criticized, the enemy's attempt to discredit a weapon he knew was powerful. Daws had countered with a warning to the fellows to use this projection only as illustration, not as actual theory.[41]

Fifty years later, however, the vast majority of the world's population is still untouched. For a while I became disenchanted,

---

[40] Betty Lee Skinner, in her book *Daws,* clarified this further. In one of Trotman's talks he said, "We counted back on one chain, and it averaged six months from the time a man started until he began to work with his man. If we extended that figure so that at the end of each six months each man took on a new man to help, in a year there'd be four, in two years there'd be sixteen. And in fifteen and a half years we'd reach the world—we'd have over two billion!...But this way, through multiplication, it would be 2,174,000,000." Betty Lee Skinner, *Daws* (Grand Rapids, MI: The Zondervan Corporation, 1974), 306.

[41] Ibid., 320.

disillusioned, and even cynical because of such schemes and, no doubt, a host of other young people joined me. It is dangerous to inspire young people with thrilling concepts that turn out to be false or at least unachievable.[42]

In the latter part of the twentieth century one mission organization worked toward world evangelization by the year 1980. In fact, the founder stated, "We are going to see the Great Commission fulfilled in this generation."[43] And he meant *his* generation.[44] But Christians failed once more. Again, just before the turn of that century, some called for the completion of world evangelization by the year 2000. What happened when it was apparent that they would not achieve their goal? The slogan was changed to "2000 and Beyond." Soon after the twenty-first century had started, this organization was disbanded.

But I must admit that even today I am proud, even grateful, to have had a vision for world evangelization as expressed in my village crusades. I still have the vision. We should never lose sight of the command the Lord has given us to go into all the world and make disciples in all nations (Matthew 28). But we must be careful in setting goals that are not inspired by the Holy Spirit. We dare not get people all hyped and have them end up disillusioned, just as I had been.

Visions and dreams like these seem to be repeated persistently. Recently some westerners got excited about the Back to Jerusalem movement circulating in China.

---

[42] As a great Dawson Trotman fan, I encourage everyone to read his biography *Daws*. It is a must read.

[43] Ken Twitchell, *Dare To Be Different* (Reading: Christian Focus Publication, 2004), 88.

[44] Ibid., 114.

Back To Jerusalem

In the 1930s and 1940s, some Chinese Christian leaders had a vision to finish the task of world evangelism by mobilizing a host of believers to evangelize the areas west of their nation and end up in Jerusalem. But then communism brought a halt to this undertaking. For some thirty-five years, the government muffled proponents of all religions in China. Christians had to go underground. Now they could only pray for survival.

Recently, however, this dream was revitalized. Young believers in unregistered churches were challenged to pick up where their fathers and grandfathers had been stopped.

Recently I received an e-mail from one of my friends. He writes:

> For the past thirteen years I have prayed and challenged our Chinese brothers and sisters here in America to take up the challenge of world evangelism. And, thank God, there have been those who have responded . . . but wait till you hear this!
>
> God is doing something spectacular in China yet so quietly behind the scenes. Let me tell you about it:
>
> It began about sixty years ago. A young Chinese Bible teacher had a burden for missionary outreach. That vision did not die even after the Communist takeover. The fire was kept alive and burst into flame about four years ago when the first Chinese missionaries went to a neighboring Buddhist country. They were followed by hundreds now working outside of China in Central Asia, South East Asia, India, the Middle East, and North Africa. The movement is known now by the name "Back to Jerusalem." It has become the driving force of the Church in China. Many feel it is the destiny to which God has called them and for which many are willing to die. One of the leaders believes that in the first decade of this movement, there may be 10,000 martyrs for Christ. It is this dedication of the Chinese church that thrills our hearts because it reflects obedience to the Great Commission.

Paul Hattaway, in his recent book, *Back to Jerusalem,* describes it this way:

> The Chinese church has no plans to rush to Israel to usher in the return of Christ. Rather, it refers to a call from God for the Chinese church to preach the gospel and establish fellowships of believers in all countries, cities, towns, and ethnic groups between China and Jerusalem. This is no small task, for within those regions lie the three largest spiritual strongholds that have yet to be conquered by the gospel: the giants of Islam, Buddhism, and Hinduism.
>
> Western mission organizations would feel they are not qualified, since none of them have ever attended seminary or have theological degrees. However, they look back confidently over their years of "prison seminary" and the lessons God taught them there.

So what is their vision? Their goal is to send up to 100,000 missionaries south and west of their borders to countries like India, Pakistan, Iran, Iraq, Syria, and other Middle Eastern countries, culminating in Jerusalem.

A spokesman of this movement stated:

> We believe the Chinese church can succeed in bringing down the religious giants of Islam, Buddhism, and Hinduism because the Lord has taught us how to work in a nation [China] where there is great opposition and persecution to the advance of the gospel. There has been great effort put into evangelizing some of the countries in the Middle East [by western missionaries], for example, but without many results. These nations are paranoid and on guard against Christianity coming from America. They have sealed their front doors as tightly shut as they can against Christianity, and they closely monitor every activity of Westerners who come to their country. While they spend all their energy guarding their front doors, maybe the Chinese Christians will quietly slip in the back door with the gospel.[45]

[45] www.backtojerusalem.com

Some acquainted with the church situation in China already have voiced concerns. They are not against a movement that may be inspired by the Lord Himself, but steps have to be taken to properly channel those forces.

Unrealistic Expectations?

Tony Lambert, director of the Overseas Missionary Fellowship's research center, and a great sympathizer of the unregistered churches in China, wrote:

> Large rural house-church networks have been enthused by the vision. They have much zeal but are hampered by lack of finance and of basic theological education, as well as lack of cross-cultural missions training. In some ways, although they have gained the most publicity overseas, their people, being mainly simple farmers, are least qualified to go overseas. . . . We are already receiving disturbing reports of some who have gone out to do evangelism to the Muslims in Xinjiang, the minorities in Yunnan and even to Moscow, who have returned disillusioned. Their unrealistic expectations have been dashed by lack of adequate training—not least in solid biblical theology which would prepare them for the hard grind of long-term cultural adaptation.[46]

Carol Hamrin, who for twenty-five years worked as the senior China research specialist at the US Department of State and is now a Research Professor at George Mason University, observed:

> The Back to Jerusalem Movement may be a good case study of the pluses and minuses. The idea of training thousands of Chinese missionaries to take the gospel to ethnic minorities, such as Tibetan Buddhist and Turkic Muslims, across China's western borders and

---

[46] www.us.omf.org

> along the Old Silk Road through Central Asia all the way back to Jerusalem is a genuine and admirable calling of the Chinese church with deep roots in the 1930s. But current efforts often reflect a simplistic and naïve response that focuses on idealistic goals and fast results more than on realistic plans.

She continues:

> For example, talk of building 10,000 training centers and sending 100,000 missionaries in ten years reflects both outside influence promoting Year 2000 goals, and Chinese millennialism. The numbers game sets idealistic inspirational goals that often dissipate in thin air. Overseas champions have added hype to the facts in their fund-raising efforts, which may be attracting enthusiasm but wasting resources without good accountability. . . . These leaders may have great faith, but there also may be a problem with irresponsibility. They may need to be challenged and helped to develop a servant leadership style.[47]

These are not criticisms of those passionate Chinese Christians, because all of us are interested in seeing the world reached for Christ. These friends of the Chinese church simply voice concerns about an endeavor that might end in total disarray unless it is channeled in the right direction.

We can only hope that this movement does not turn into another pipe dream. What we have seen so far in commitment, faith, boldness, dedication, and vision is admirable. But it dare not keep on just sounding great or just remain interesting to easily hyped people who usually perform great on the surface but generally lack depth in understanding and execution.

---

[47] Carol Lee Hamrin, "The Global Chinese: Rethinking Kingdom-Building and Nation-Building," given as a keynote address in Virginia Beach, Virginia on September 17, 2003.

I am totally committed to the Great Commission. We all have to be. May God answer the prayers of committed, visionary believers so that this dream may not end like so many other man-made attempts. As partners in the gospel it is our responsibility to help train the emerging young Christian leaders in China. They have much to teach us in commitment, fervor, zeal, passion, and enthusiasm, but as partners with them we can help them be realistic, get solid biblical schooling, and gird them with our prayerful support wherever it is needed.

Chapter 9

Secret Orders, Falun Gong, and Jesus

Stability is the watchword of the Chinese government now. Throughout Chinese history, rulers had to fend off opponents who were seen as threats to the ruling class. Often such threats came from those who were bred by secret orders where they initially felt secure. Emperors ruled with an iron fist to ward off such threats and succeeded only through sheer force and rigorous willpower. They indiscriminately sacrificed lives in order to stay in power. Leaders who began their intrigues within the safety of such secret orders sometimes shook and overthrew dynasties. That is why government officials always have been and are—even up to this day—suspicious of those who live, work, and worship clandestinely.

Secret Orders

Mao Zedong was one of many such Chinese leaders. In his wake up to 50 million (some say up to 70 million) Chinese lost their lives.

This is not only a Chinese phenomenon, however. We find brutal rulers throughout history. But what makes this so frightening is their existence in our day. Despots such as Stalin, Hitler, Fidel Castro, Idi Amin, Pol Pot, Milosevic, and Sadam Hussein all lived in the twentieth century. All of them developed a fierce apparatus of secret surveillance to help them rule by terror and fear. Rulers spied upon secret orders or groups, incarcerating or executing many of their leaders.

China, with its civilization lasting 4,000 or 5,000 years, has had to cope with such realities. Dubious leaders repeatedly emerged from nowhere. One of those leaders was Zhu Yuanzhang. He was born into a poor family in 1328. For a short time he lived in a monastery and earned his livelihood by begging and stealing. Then he disappeared in a secret order whose members believed in and looked forward to the reincarnation of Maitreya-Buddha. They hoped for a savior who would lead them out of poverty into a glorious and prosperous future.

As a thirty-nine-year old, Zhu became the paramount leader of this order, assembled an army, and eventually overthrew the emperor in Beijing (the north capital) in 1367. He established a new dynasty (Ming 1368–1644) and chose Nanjing (the south capital in place of Beijing, the north capital) to become the new capital. In order to retain power, he distanced himself from his secret order and massacred many of his former associates. He became one of the most brutal despots China had seen up to that time. Sixteen emperors followed, however, sustaining and expanding the dynasty Zhu had founded. They reigned during one of the longest and most stable dynasties in Chinese history.

From time to time new secret orders emerged and played havoc with the rulers in power. One of the most dangerous threats came from Hong Xiuquan (1814–64), who was born in poverty like so many before him. He met Christian missionaries in the southern part of China and later proclaimed himself to be the brother of Jesus Christ. As the new "messiah" he was to lead an impoverished nation toward a new heaven on earth. He called it "the heavenly kingdom of great peace" and ruled for fifteen years. The Taiping Rebellion (1850–64) under his leadership claimed over 20 million lives and finally was put down with the help of foreign powers. He ended his life by committing suicide.

Throughout Chinese history the governments in power always fought back when someone challenged their authority. Sometimes they succeeded, other times they did not. Even the Buddhists suffered a setback when Tang Dynasty emperors (ninth century) ordered all Buddhist monasteries shut down.

Tony Lambert had this to say:

> Control of religious affairs in China is not a recent innovation by the Chinese Communist Party (CCP)....the "Son of Heaven" ruled supreme. Popular folk religion was tolerated but looked down on by the urbane and quasi-agnostic Confucian officials. Secret societies and religious sects that multiplied and became hotbeds of sedition were ruthlessly suppressed. They were *xie*—"heterodox"—beyond the pale of Confucian orthodoxy.[48]

Falun Gong

Because of such a history, Chinese governments are always wary of unchecked spiritual organizations or secret orders. Falun Gong is the most recent one. Founded by Li Hongzhi, born in northern China on July 7, 1952, this sectarian association grew rapidly and now has millions of followers around the world. Both of his parents were medical doctors. As a young man he dabbled in traditional folk religions. The revival of Buddhism and Taoism after the disastrous Cultural Revolution brought forth teachers and masters in this field to influence searching people who felt betrayed by the Communist Party. Young Li was greatly influenced by such teachers. He felt called to search for truth, which he then wanted to share with others.

This he did in his own way. He founded Falun Gong, which embraces teachings that incorporated five meditative movements

---

[48] The Present Religious Policy of the Chinese Communist Party, OMF, *Religion, State & Society* 39, no. 3, 2001.

developed from primordial Chinese techniques such as Qigong.[49] Such teachings in spiritual healing and illumination were an antidote to communistic propaganda that had proven meaningless and often detrimental to society. In order to operate legally, groups like Falun Gong simply established a Qigong school, became an accepted member of the official Qigong association, and operated under this safe umbrella. Many disgusted, misled Chinese flocked to seminars and discussion groups to absorb methods and systems that apparently could fill that void. Li successfully combined some of the traditional teachings of Taoism, Buddhism, and even Christianity into a new belief.

He quickly rose to prominence when Chinese from all strata of society, including members of the Communist Party, became ardent and zealous followers. Leaders of the party saw this as a threat and turned against this new association.

On April 25, 1999, thousands of Falun Gong adherents assembled in Beijing to demonstrate against the government's ban of this movement. Li had left the day before for overseas, where he had planned to lecture. He now lives in New York and has become a US citizen. From his new headquarters he directs and oversees his worldwide movement.

He authored a book *Zhuan Falun* (The Dharma-wheel), which has been translated into nine languages. By using the technique of Qigong, which can be achieved by certain exercises lasting some twenty minutes, plus embracing truthfulness, goodness, and tolerance, master Li enables people by long distance to get the Dharma-wheel moving again in one's lower body. This supposedly guarantees protection, and through this miracle a person is safe from all harm and becomes invulnerable. It is said that Li has become a multimillionaire.

---

[49] This term was invented by the People's Republic of China in the early 1950s to embrace accepted practices used by adherents of Taoism and traditional medicine to lift the quality of life.

The authorities in China soon came out with new guidelines to rein in this and other potential superstitious cults. Any organization shall be identified as a cult, if it:

1. sets up illegal organizations in the name of religion;
2. defies its leaders;
3. manufactures and distributes superstitions and heresies;
4. instigates and deceives people and recruits and controls the members by means of manufactured superstitions and heresies;
5. is systematically involved in activities disturbing public order and endangering the security of citizens' lives and property.

The Chinese government is extremely suspicious of Christian groups as well, but only those that meet in secret and are not willing to register. The government sees this as a violation of its laws. The Religious Affairs Bureau oversees all religions in China. Five religions have special status in China: Buddhism, Taoism, Islam, Protestantism, and Catholicism. Other religions are under consideration. Rules, regulations, and guidelines have been established to give some constancy to these groups and to keep them toeing the line of the Communist Party.

It is well known that atheists presently rule China. Its leaders proudly proclaim and vigorously defend their convictions. In return they recognize and accept the convictions other countries hold, whether they are guided by other nonbeliefs or beliefs such as found in Islamic, Christian, Hindu, or animist countries. China prides itself in atheistic socialism with Chinese characteristics. Their ultimate goal is to have all citizens accept socialism as the best ideology and political system for China. Even Bishop Ting writes:

> In this stage of history, we [China] are constructing socialism. For China, socialism is much more capable, as a social system, of embodying love than capitalism. . . . It enables humankind to achieve

> a level of equality never seen before. The universalization of love is the goal of socialism. Socialism is love on a large scale, organized love, love which has taken shape as a social system.[50]

The Chinese government wants all religions in China to adapt their beliefs to mirror this view. In line with the present Chinese constitution, however, citizens are not forced to become atheists, nor should they be forced to embrace religious beliefs. Let me state again: This has been enshrined in the Chinese constitution.

Anti-Government Remarks

In my many years of ministry in China I have yet to find a Christian who has been incarcerated because of his or her beliefs. I do not say that this has never happened in China. Others insist that this has happened many times. If it is done, however, believers do have legal rights to defend themselves. Other China observers may not agree with me, but we cannot ignore the changes that have occurred. In fact, change continues to occur in China. The government has begun to invite foreign legal experts to help them develop a strong legal system. Hopefully this will lead to more understanding of human rights.

What often is branded as persecution is de facto prosecution. Let me explain.

I am often asked about Chinese Christians under siege. Let me give you an example of so-called persecution. I met with a middle-aged Chinese in California who had found the Lord in China just a few years ago. He is closely linked to the house church movement and now lives in the United States.

He told me about Li Ming (not his real name), a personal acquaintance of his. Li is a Chinese house-church leader and "historian," who

---

[50] See chapter on The Role of Theological Education.

was sentenced to two years of *laojiao* (re-education through labor) by the Re-education Through Labor Commission of Ping Ding Shan County in Henan Province. In the process of my interview, he admitted that Li had written anti-government statements in his journal. Those are grounds for detention in China. This, of course, would be unacceptable in a truly democratic country. In China, however, when any anti-government remarks are made—whether in public or in private—they will be prosecuted.

This is confirmed by Sydney Rittenberg in his fascinating book *The Man Who Stayed Behind.* As an American GI during the Second World War, he was sent to China in 1945. A devout communist from North Carolina, he decided to remain in China to help rebuild that nation. He met Mao and became convinced that he was the right man to lift China from its ashes and to free it from imperialism. He became a zealot and a true follower of the Great Helmsman. He understood that no one dared to cross or criticize Mao, even when criticism was voiced to help the cause. He wrote:

> The Lushan conference at which Peng Dehuai had been removed was followed by a campaign against right opportunists. That meant anyone in the party who had expressed doubts about the Great Leap Forward [Mao's disastrous program in 1958 to transform China's economy]. At the Broadcast Administration, one of the first targets was my gentle friend Ding Yilan. Capable, kind, and almost painfully honest, she had made the mistake of sharing her diary entries at a party meeting. In her diary, she had fretted that the aging Mao was losing control of himself, growing increasingly arbitrary and dictatorial, and even losing his ability to listen to other people's opinions. After a struggle meeting, she was sent to a farm in Hebei Province for a year of hard labor.[51]

---

[51] Sydney Rittenberg, *The Man Who Stayed Behind* (New York: Simon and Schuster, 1993), 249.

According to the gentleman I interviewed, Li made further statements in writing, such as "We ask the Lord to destroy the strongholds in China," and wrote prayers to destroy atheistic organizations in China. This, of course, is anathema to the Chinese government.

Even though millions of Christians freely worship in China, others are seen by the government as potential threats. Who are they? Li is such a person. Whenever things are done secretly, the authorities become suspicious and nervous. Li is paying the consequences of his anti-government stance as expressed in his private writings. But it must be clearly said that his incarceration is not based upon him being a Christian.

Strange Teachings

Young, theologically uneducated men and women often lead a number of groups that do not register with the government. These leaders may gain prominence because of their charismatic personalities. Combine this lack of theological training with distorted teachings, and bizarre groups will result.

One such leader announced he was the brother of Jesus. To become a follower, you have to be filled with the Holy Spirit. How is this achieved? He teaches that the Holy Spirit passes from him to another whenever someone has sex with him.

Other similar yet terrible incidents happened in the province of Hubei. Rev. Wang and his wife Rev. Ge are dedicated church leaders in Wuhan. He is the principal of the theological seminary in that city, while his wife is one of the great evangelists in China. They have trained hundreds of emerging young Christian leaders over the years. Hearing what happened to two former students shocked and saddened them.

"South Korean 'missionaries' taught that true spirituality can be achieved only through forty days of fasting and prayer," they told us on our last visit to Wuhan. "Two of our former students fell under the spell of their teaching. One of them died on the thirty-sixth day of a fast. She did not make it, and the other did not either."

"How is that possible?" I asked in disbelief.

"It got even worse," they continued. "The false teacher assured them, 'Don't worry. They will be raised from the dead on the third day.'"

Christian workers like Wang and Rev. Ge encounter similar episodes all the time. "No wonder the political authorities are at odds with Christians who spread such teachings," they sighed.

Another led a group of followers on top of a mountain in the Guangdong province. The leader told them that on a given day Jesus would return and take these believers to Himself. Everyone gave away all of his belongings, dressed in white garb, and climbed the mountain. When Jesus did not appear, the local authorities had to feed and house these misled people and then transport them back to their home villages.

This so enraged the authorities that they are leery whenever someone teaches or preaches on the Second Coming of Christ. Not being theologians, they do not know much about Christian teachings. They can't discern true and false doctrine. All they see is the bad fruit of teachings given by uneducated, misinformed, and strange "Christian leaders."

Then there was Ji Sanbao, who is convinced he is the incarnation of Jesus Christ. He chose twelve men to be his disciples, and thus the sect is called "The Disciples." He claims to have brought sight to the blind, made the lame to walk, and even brought a dead woman back to life. The sect, which has spread across twelve provinces, maintains over one million adherents.[52]

Cults and sects shoot up like mushrooms all over China. "There are the Shouters and the Spirit Church, the Disciples Association and White Sun, the Holistic Church and the Crying Faction. Many are apocalyptic. A few are strongly anti-communist. The Grades

---

[52] Georg Zimmermann, *StuDeO INFO* (September 2003).

of Servants and Eastern Lightning[53] are among the largest, each claiming membership in the millions."[54]

The appeal of sects is astonishing. On November 25, 2004, the *New York Times* reported on the rigorous methods and bizarre teachings of cultic leaders to win converts.

> Xu Shuangfu, who the authorities say was born Su Wenkou, is a religious entrepreneur. Now in his sixties, he founded Three Grades of Servants in Henen Province in the late 1980s and oversaw its growth despite serving time in custody.
>
> The sect's hierarchy is based on what Mr. Xu argued is the theme of a trinity that runs through Scripture, including three servants of God (Moses, Aaron, and Pashur, the ancestor of a priestly family) in the Old Testament, and three friends of Jesus (Martha, Mary, and Lazarus) in the New Testament. Mr. Su [*sic*] occupies the top grade and maintains that he, as Moses did, talks to God.
>
> The group is millenarian. Mr. Xu, followers say, predicted that Jesus would return to earth and eliminate nonbelievers in 1989, then again in 1993. When this did not happen, Mr. Xu explained that even God misjudged how long Abraham's descendents would stay in Egypt. He did not set a third date for the Second Coming.

It is no wonder that cults thrive in this environment. The best antidote for lies and deception is to present the truth of God's Word. Contrary to what some may believe about this nation, "the word of God is not bound" (2 Tim. 2:9 KJV).

---

[53] Eastern Lightning was founded in 1990 by a woman called Deng, claiming to be the returned Christ.

[54] *New York Times*, "China's Poor, Seeking Solace in Personal Religion, Are Caught in Violence," November 25, 2004.

Forbidden Topics?

Critics claim that the Books of Daniel and Revelation are no-no's for preachers in China because of end-time prophecies. Cynics have even told me that Bibles printed in China do not contain those two books. I have yet to see one Bible printed in China without those two books. A number of evangelical leaders representing anti-China organizations broadcast distortions like these around the world. I repeatedly run into misled Christians in the West who believe such stories.

One of our teaching team members preached about Christ's return. A spiritually hungry crowd filled the church in Wuhan on this bright and sunny morning. Not knowing his topic in advance, I was stunned yet pleased when our preacher announced the theme of his sermon.

Without hesitation he gave a wonderful discourse on the Second Coming of Christ. *What will our Chinese friends say?* I wondered. *Isn't this a forbidden topic according to some of my western friends?*

Western China watchers had often warned me about communist spies sitting in all congregations to report on the preaching. I did not mind and always thanked God for unbelievers who sat under my preaching. Where else would they hear a clear presentation of the gospel?

This morning could be the turning point of our teaching and preaching ministry. If preaching on the Second Coming of Christ was forbidden in China, then we would be in trouble—deep trouble.

After the service the senior pastor approached me with a big smile, thanking me for the good sermon. "This is our hope!" he exclaimed, "We all look forward to that great day when Jesus will return and we will have the joy of reigning with Him forever."

As long as teaching and preaching are done properly, and based upon the Bible, no one has to feel hampered in proclaiming truth.

In all of my preaching experiences, I never had to hand in the manuscript or outlines of my sermons beforehand. And I had the privilege and joy to preach from Shenyang in the north to Guangzhou in the south, from Chengdu in the west to Hangzhou in the east. Nor have I ever been reprimanded or challenged on anything that I had said or taught. I always had total freedom in selecting my topics and preaching from the Word of God. So did all of the members on the China Partner teaching teams.

As the Scriptures are preached faithfully, the Chinese will gain an accurate understanding of Jesus Christ. Historically this has not always happened, resulting in syncretism. China Partner works to uphold a biblical view of the person and work of Christ to the Chinese people.

The Face Of Jesus In China

What do the Chinese mainly think of Jesus? How do they visualize Him? What kind of a picture do they draw of Him, and how has the picture changed throughout the centuries?

In his research on this topic, Roman Malek[55] describes how Nestorian monks (the first one was Jaballus) from eastern Syria traveled along the Silk Road and reached the Chinese capital of that time in AD 635. It was the first time that Christians had entered Changan, today's Xian.

The Emperor Taizong (AD 626–49) was greatly interested in their Christian teachings. He even permitted monasteries to be built in the capital city and later across some provinces as well. Missionary endeavors were undertaken without restraint throughout the land. It is believed that with the help of Buddhist scholars their religious writings were translated into Chinese. Interestingly, they translated God or Jesus with *Tianzun,* meaning heavenly ruler, which

[55] Roman Malek researched this in depth. His findings are chronicled in *Monumenta Serica Monograph* Series L/1, Volume 1, jointly published by Institut Monumenta Serica and China-Zentrum Sankt Augustin, Steyler Verlag, Nettetal, 2002. *The Chinese Face of Jesus Christ.*

was the name of honor for Buddha. Thus Jesus received His first Chinese face.

Visiting China today you can readily buy a lithographic print of the famous Nestorian stone monument. The believers of the Nestorian church chiseled this monument in AD 781. On this slab of granite you can decipher a Christian text and the life story of Jesus as redeemer. Over the years, however, the basic and fundamental teachings of Jesus' suffering and His crucifixion seemed to have vanished. Only 146 years after the first monks had reached Xian, the face of Jesus had been transformed into a "radiating sun" that manipulates the helm of the *Boat of Compassion* and steers it to the *Palace of Light*. Furthermore, the Nestorian cross grows out of a lotus flower. Jesus and Buddha find each other. In other words, they embrace each other. The crucified Jesus had become a buddhistic-taoistic messiah.

Fourteen hundred years have passed since the Nestorian Chinese Christians had developed their own unique face of Jesus. The face of Jesus continued to change. The Chinese continuously tried to picture Him in new ways. They asked whether Jesus needed to be seen as a redeemer, or if they should reject Him as a charlatan, a barbarian, or even as a criminal.

Was Jesus to be seen as a friend or adversary of Confucius? Should He be seen as an opponent of Laozi and Buddha? Or was He a social reformer, a rebel, or revolutionary? Was He even a precursor to Marx and Mao?

Or was Jesus to be seen as a *junzi*, a noble and exemplary man?

No doubt Jesuits like Michele Ruggieri (1543–1607) and Matteo Ricci (1552–1610) confused the situation further. They were great scholars and accepted by the court in Beijing; however, they blurred the understanding of the true Jesus by wanting to make Him acceptable to the Chinese within their own culture. Matteo Ricci purposely tried to minimize the importance of Jesus' suffering and crucifixion in order to blend Christian beliefs with Confucian thought. He tried to glorify Jesus as the noble and good person who is worth accepting and following. In a sense, now Jesus and Confucius embraced each other.

C. P. Fitzgerald wrote this about Ricci's first encounter with the Chinese emperor in Beijing:

> In 1601, after a delay of two years, his gifts were offered to the Emperor, and the incident is thus recorded by Chinese historians:
> In the second month the eunuch Ma Tang of T'ien Ts'in brought to the Court Li Ma-tou [Ricci], a man from the western ocean, who had some rare gifts for the Emperor. The Emperor sent the eunuch's memorial to the Board of Rites who replied:
> "The western ocean countries have had no relations with us, and do not accept our laws. The images and paintings of the Lord of Heaven and of a virgin which Li Ma-tou offers as tribute are not of great value. He offers a purse in which he says there are the bones of immortals, as if the immortals, when they ascend to heaven did not take their bones with them. On a similar occasion Han Yü [The great T'ang scholar and anti-Buddhist. The occasion referred to is, no doubt, the offering of a reputed finger of Buddha to the Emperor mentioned in Chapter XVI] said that one should not allow such novelties to be introduced into the palace for fear of bringing misfortune. We advise, therefore, that his presents should not be received, and he should not be permitted to remain in the capital. He should be sent back to his own country."
> In spite of this decision, the emperor received the presents and permitted Li Ma-tou to live at the capital.
> This entry is typical and illuminating. The Confucian Board of Rites took up a strictly traditional opposition to all foreign novelties, while the Court tolerated the foreigner in just the same way as the T'ang Emperors had tolerated the foreign religious wanderers of the eighth and ninth centuries. No doubt, Father Ricci, with his relics and images of the saints, seemed to the Chinese indistinguishable from the innumerable very similarly equipped

> Buddhist monks who had from time to time sought Court protection for their particular deities. Ricci remained in Peking [Beijing], where he died in 1610.[56]

Malek points out that the face of Jesus became terribly distorted when around 1850 Hong Xiuquan (1814–64) declared himself as the younger brother of Jesus. He wanted to be the new messiah for China and the rest of the world. As instigator and leader of the Taiping Rebellion, he managed to occupy Nanjing but was quickly defeated with the help of foreign troops. Even today certain religious Christian fanatics claim to be Jesus Himself or at least brothers of His.

Strangely, even the Communists tried in some way to make Jesus fit into their misguided, some say demonic, ideology. After the communist revolution—or liberation as they try to portray it—the victorious leaders published a newsletter in which they stated that the "Realization of Communism is the Fulfillment of the Hope of Jesus." With this, Jesus became the face of a proletarian revolutionary.

It got even worse. The firebrands and misled youngsters of the Cultural Revolution (1966–76) elevated Marx and Mao to the rank of Jesus, thus announcing a new trinity. "Chairman Jesus" received a new face, and this time Mao and Jesus embraced. The words of Mao were collected in the form of a Bible—the "red bible."

What then will be the final face of Jesus? Having traveled across China for many years, I believe that Jesus has finally regained the face we see depicted in the Holy Scriptures. If Chinese believers are to preach Christ, they cannot do it apart from His Word. Theological education is of paramount importance for the survival of Christ's church in China. We shall devote our attention to this pressing need in more detail in the next chapter.

---

[56] C. P. Fitzgerald, *China, A Short Cultural History* (Boulder and London: Westview Press, 1985), 481.

Chapter 10

The Role of Theological Education

Ever since the opening of China to the rest of the world, concerned Christians have been anxious to pick up the trail where faithful missionaries had left off. With great love and much enthusiasm, many of them traveled to China to see for themselves what had happened and what might be done to help the cause of Christ. Finding a vibrant church stunned them. They had expected to find a few struggling believers, but not a strong reemerging and thriving church! As so often in history, God had done what very few of His people could envision.

Twenty-six years have passed since the reopening of the first church in Ningbo (Zhejiang) in 1979. Since then over 17,000 churches have registered, thereby receiving permission by local authorities to carry on their diverse and manifold Christian ministries. Six churches are being added or opened every single day. Furthermore, between 30,000 and 40,000 groups of believers, who gather at what are called meeting points affiliated with the Three-Self Patriotic Movement (TSPM)/China Christian Council (CCC), await their turn at registration. Most of these groups meet in homes, public meeting halls, or wherever they find room. Most of them are small, but some of them number in the hundreds, even up to 1,000 worshipers or more.

This is a remarkable development. In Western thinking, all of those so-called meeting points or house churches would be considered churches. A minimum of 50,000 recognized churches exist in China today. These do not include the multitudes of non-registered house churches spread across the land.

A Great Need

Our Chinese friends can give us some great insights into the role of theological education and how it affects their churches and the society in which they live out their Christian faith. I regret that I cannot speak for the many house churches that did not register with the local authorities. Very little is in print as to how they see the importance of theological education. It is known that they make great efforts to train their constituents in mostly covert undertakings.

With the explosion of church growth in China, unprecedented in the history of Christianity, many churches are in serious trouble. Lacking competent and biblically trained pastors, churches are prone to fall into heretical teaching. This is especially true in the house church movement. Many of them mix their Christian belief with folk religions. Therefore the training of emerging young leaders is of utmost importance. Wang Aiming, vice president of Nanjing Union Theological Seminary, laments, "At present the reality of pastoring believers in grassroots churches is far from meeting the demands of the truth of the gospel. The basic problem is that theology is not broad enough to the point that many evangelists simply have no idea of theology."[57]

[57] Wang Aiming, "The Nature and Purpose of Theological Reconstruction in the Chinese Church," *Chinese Theological Review* 15 (2001): 24.

Yan Xiyu, former instructor at the Sichuan Theological Seminary, writes:

> Many co-workers in the church today tire themselves out with busyness; they are like a fire brigade running off to the next place. They have no vision. Of course, there are many reasons why this situation arose, but the poverty of theology is a crucial element. In our church exists to a greater or lesser extent, faith that is Christian in name but not in substance. Poverty of thinking can make a person appear shallow, impetuous, lost. In the same way, poverty of theology will make a church appear foundationless, easily shaken by the winds of heresy. [58]

Theological education plays a key role in a changing church and society in China. Historical, theological, and missiological components affect what is happening in China today in the realm of theological education.

Historical

Compared to the two most accepted religions, Buddhism[59] and Taoism, Christianity did not enjoy quick acceptance by the Chinese general public for centuries. According to official tradition, Buddhism entered from India in the first century AD. Taoism was home grown. Therefore for centuries Chinese scholars did few studies on Christianity—they simply did not have any interest in that religion. Only recently has the church made great strides in winning the favor

---

[58] Yan Xiyu, "What is Theology?" *Chinese Theological Review* 15 (2001): 40–41.

[59] "The Chinese of the time adopted Buddha into their scheme of things as a demigod on the order of their own mythical Yellow Emperor and the philosopher Lao Tzu, who was believed to have attained immortality. But the dawn of history for Chinese Buddhism comes with the rendition of Buddhist sacred texts into the Chinese language." William Theodore de Bary, ed., *Sources of Chinese Tradition*, vol. 1 (New York: Columbia University, 1960), 272–73.

of people in all strata of society. Interestingly, the greatest advance Christianity made was—and still is—under a communist regime, even though the mass media and several evangelical groups have informed us for years that Christianity in China is under siege.

Today secular scholars in China take great interest in Christianity, particularly the development of the burgeoning church. The Institute of World Religions of the Chinese Academy of Social Sciences, a think tank, reports directly to the government. Within this department a "Center for Research of Christianity" was formed in 1998. Visiting scholars from overseas who declare themselves as Christians are now allowed to work at this center.

Zhuo Xinping, present director of the Institute for Christian Studies and director of the Institute of World Religions in Beijing, sheds some light on this subject:

> Research in Christianity by Chinese scholars began in the late Ming (sixteenth century) and Qing (seventeenth to early twentieth century) Dynasties. The debate between missionaries and the Chinese literati of the time over the relationship between Christianity and Chinese thought and culture—Christ versus Confucius, orthodoxy versus heresy, Chinese versus barbarian, along with the rites controversy and the term question—both stimulated and influenced the study of Christianity on many levels and from many perspectives. In the 1950s and 1960s, scholarly circles in China engaged in related research in history, philosophy, intercultural exchange, and investigation of social conditions. Since the late 1970s, contemporary studies in Christianity in China have entered the stage of systematic inquiry, and substantive achievements have been realized.[60]

Note that this statement comes from a non-Christian scholar related to an institute that is endorsed and run by an atheistic government.

---

[60] Zhuo Xinping, "The Study of Christianity in China Today," *Chinese Theological Review* 15 (2001): 1.

Before 1949, about twenty Christian universities functioned in China. The Communist Party and/or government seized all of them. Some studies on religion continued until the Cultural Revolution (1966–76), when all religious activities ceased, and then picked up again in the 1980s.

Presently, so writes Zhuo Xinping:

> Chinese scholars' study of religion for the most part includes the history of world Christianity, Christian theology, philosophy, aesthetics, ethical thought, the study of the Bible, the history of Christianity in China, the study of major denominations and their mission boards and missionary religious orders, the current state and trends in the development of Christianity, the study of Christian organizations and famous personages, the study of Christian art and culture, and so on.[61]

He continues in stating other interests:

> The development of Protestantism in China, Christianity since the Republican era, Chinese attitudes toward Christianity, and the attack on and defense of religion (including "missionary cases," the anti-Christian movement, and so on), the relationship between Christianity and Chinese culture, the history of Christian colleges in China, the indigenization of Christianity and the Three-Self Patriotic Movement, along with catalogues of historical documents relating to Christianity in China. But overall the study of Christianity in China is still at the stage of collecting materials, individual case studies, and introductory historical studies. [62]

In the past several years, beginning with 1997, it seems that Christianity is experiencing the same process of sinicizing as Buddhism did in the Tang Dynasty—mainly during the fifth and sixth century.

---

[61] Ibid., 7.

[62] Ibid., 8.

When it comes to sinicization or indigenization, Zhuo Xinping concludes:

> In addition, in the discussion of issues around the developmental trend of Chinese Christianity the terminology for "sinicization of Christianity" or "indigenization" is not uniform, and bias on both sides is marked. One group believes that the integrity of the Chinese church and its theology demands that it rids itself of the influence in the modern era of Western missionaries and their theological thinking, methods, and language, and engage with Chinese culture in order to realize their goal of an "indigenous church" or "indigenous theology." The other side feels that the very terms "sinicization" or "indigenization" in themselves are misunderstandings of the true nature of Christianity. In their view Christianity is not a question of "sinicization" or "indigenization." They suggest that an understanding of communicating the Christian message should have a holistic basis. They propose to substitute "contextualization" and "mother-tongue" theology for the term "indigenization," and in the context of China put their efforts into the construction and the development of "theology in Chinese."[63]

According to Rev. Su Deci, former general secretary of the CCC and present president of the East China Theological Seminary in Shanghai, theological education in China had its beginning in 1850. Missionaries had emphasized theological education after church planting, and about sixty theological institutions existed in China before the great exodus of missionaries. Because the Chinese church had relied heavily on financial support, theological education then became a daunting task, as the principles of Three-Self (self-government, self-support, and self-propagation) were put into effect thus stopping the financial support from overseas. Trials also brought blessings, however, one of them being the uniting of the church. But enrollment declined, and the government closed all institutions

[63] Ibid., 8–9.

during the Cultural Revolution. With the introduction of new policies of religious freedom in the early 1980s, schools reopened. The lesson of how to incorporate Christian theology into Chinese soil propelled theological education forward.

As of 2004, twenty-three theological institutions besides a number of lay-leader schools are scattered across China. They can be categorized into four levels: national, regional, provincial, and grassroots schools. About 2,000 students are enrolled in the first three levels, and over 5,000 students have graduated over the years. About 250 instructors, 80 percent of whom are graduates of the past twenty years, teach these students.

The great need is to improve the quality of theological education by upgrading the faculties. Only one-third of them have theological degrees. The curriculum for seminaries has to be improved as well. The goal is to improve education by the year 2015, paying special attention to the demands of liturgy and pastoral care. Our Chinese friends see a fourfold function of theological education: instruction, research, social ministry, and communication of the gospel and biblical truth.

Chinese Christians want to develop their own theology. This does not necessarily mean that they want to move away from historical, biblical beliefs but want to consider the importance of Chinese culture.

Theological

Theological education in China plays a vital role in the spiritual development of the mushrooming churches. After the reemergence of the church in China following the catastrophic Cultural Revolution, the emphasis was first placed on opening and renovating church buildings and reestablishing theological training centers such as seminaries and Bible schools. In those early years, pastors who had spent many years in exile—working on farms, in factories and/or mines—mainly taught theology. Very few of them were scholars, but they had a deep passion to train the young emerging Christian leaders how to run the church well. Most of them had studied in seminaries during the period of missionary involvement when theology rooted in western thinking was taught. Thus western theological thinking saturated much of what they taught.

Now the church in China stands at a crossroads. Some Christian leaders want to indigenize or bring about the sinicization of their present theology. As long as it is done within the framework of biblical truths, churches will not suffer. If it moves away from it, however, as was done by liberal theologians in Germany (as a German I want to refrain from accusing theologians of other nationalities), then alarm bells should ring. I have cautioned my Chinese friends to look at the result of liberal theology in Europe where liberalism emptied our churches.

Many Chinese and non-Chinese theologians, scholars, and grassroots Christians were disturbed after reading Bishop Ting's book *Love Never Ends*. All persons interested in the development of the church in China, however, must be willing to grapple with the intricacies of Chinese culture, history, and politics before criticizing someone who has the Chinese church at heart. The church in China cannot and must not be seen in simple black and white.

On the other hand, any scholar such as Bishop Ting, the foremost Chinese Christian liberal thinker and theologian of our times, is interested in the critique of other scholars, no matter whether it comes from those within or outside of China. Some matters concern those who accept the Bible as the very foundation of their faith. What are some of those concerns?

Justification by Love?

Bishop Ting is genuinely interested in the survival of the Chinese church and its important role in the consolidation of Chinese socialist society. Apparently he considers socialism with Chinese characteristics as the epitome of political development. But is socialism really the force that can bring an end to a suffering people? He agrees with evangelical believers that God's redemptive grace is necessary for the salvation of man; however, he stresses the process of self-realization of man through efforts of love. Sin receives a new definition. It is no longer only transgression of God's law but a neglect of fellow human beings who were sinned against by exploitation and oppression. The bishop puts forth the mixing of social and salvational liberation.

Furthermore, he suggests that man's fall has not depraved man completely. Much remained in man that is positive as exemplified in expressions of truth, love, and beauty. He favors Justin Martyr's dictum "that in every person born, no matter who, there is the seed of the Logos—the Word."[64]

Therefore we must ask for clarification on a number of concerns. Is justification by love taught in Scripture? Do our works grant us a more glorious future? Is there any judgment resulting in condemnation? If there is a heaven, is there a hell? Is the primary task of the church propagation or proclamation (*kerygma*) and the secondary task service (*diakonia*)? Is it patriotic to be for socialism but not for free enterprise? What about the strong emphasis on the theory of a Cosmic Christ?[65]

Though subscribing to the Apostolic and Nicene Creeds, Bishop Ting seems willing to depart somewhat from traditional teachings of the universal church.

The Chinese original version of the bishop's book was published under the title *Selected Writings of K. H. Ting*. The editor for the English translation, Janice Wickerie, states, "*Love Never Ends* [thus] fulfills in some way the expressed need among church leaders in China for an intellectual expression of Christianity which

---

[64] K. H. Ting, *Love Never Ends* (Nanjing: Nanjing Amity Printing Co., Ltd., 1998), 243.

[65] Ibid., 424.

can stand on a par with the new interest in Christianity—as a philosophical and moral theory, and sometimes as a faith—among Chinese intellectuals since the mid-1980s."[66]

In other words, Chinese theologians and some pastors are concerned about the potential shallowness of Christian believers unless they are encouraged to drive their roots into Chinese society as is now experienced. They live in a socialist society and therefore must be willing to make their witness understood by their fellow citizens. Bishop Ting states, "We in China want our church and theology to take root in the Chinese soil, and guard the concept of sin both from its simplistic denial by humanist optimism and its unwarranted universalization in the name of orthodoxy."[67]

Theological Reconstruction

Bishop Ting encourages the development of a Chinese theology. The term used for this purpose is "theological reconstruction" or as others put it "reconstruction of theological thinking." After repeated negative reactions toward those terms, some Christian leaders in China changed it to "theological thinking construction." The intent remains the same, however.

The bishop wants input from Chinese grassroots Christians as well as theologians and intellectuals. Some of his ideas were and are still debated in the West, such as social exegesis; openness theology (God's freedom); God's nature of love; His continuous work of creation, redemption, and sanctification; and progress theology. Chinese Christians, as well as all Christians, have to be willing to debate these matters honestly and without discrimination—especially in light of biblical truth. Will they withstand the scrutiny of those who have the highest respect for biblical integrity?

In light of the demise of socialism in European and non-European countries, overseas Christians may be disturbed by Bishop Ting's

---

[66] Janice Wickerie, "Editor's Note for the English Version," *Love Never Ends,* 10.
[67] Ting, *Love Never Ends,* 147.

conviction that "In this stage of history, we [China] are constructing socialism. For China, socialism is much more capable, as a social system, of embodying love than capitalism. . . . It enables humankind to achieve a level of equality never seen before. The universalization of love is the goal of socialism. Socialism is love on a large scale, organized love, love which has taken shape as a social system."[68]

What has this to do with theology or the biblical mandate? For many Chinese Christians it has a lot to do with it. They are interested in winning their fellow citizens to Christ. For them it is consequential to be understood by them. Chinese, who put great emphasis on relationships, feel strongly that they can get the attention of non-Christians only by living exemplary lives. It is not so much what you say that counts, but what you do or how you behave. "Show me how you behave, and I will show you what you believe," is their axiom. We may call it lifestyle evangelism. For the Christians in China, however, it has become a way of life. Socialism is not necessarily a political policy or scheme to fear but a social system in which they are forced to live—and many of them readily do.

An essay by a seminar professor encouraged me regarding this process. He stated:

> The significance of theological reconstruction is first of all to guarantee that in the twenty-first century Chinese Christians' faith will be understood by the Chinese people to guarantee that the Chinese church continues to advance and prosper in taking up its given responsibility and duty, and to guarantee that what the church preaches is orthodox and pure faith and doctrine. Second, the realization of theological reconstruction means that the Chinese churches' reputation and prestige in the church ecumenical will finally be established. Third, it means that no heresy or heterodox preaching will find any way to mislead the millions of Chinese Christians.[69]

---

[68] Ibid., 219.

[69] Wang, "Theological Reconstruction," 25–26.

Yan Xiyu, former instructor at the Sichuan Theological Seminary, has this to say:

> Theological reflection helps purify our Christian faith. Our faith is always guided by theological thinking; faith without theological guidance does not exist. Because of a long absence of conscious theological reflection in the Chinese church, the purity of Christian faith is subject today to the attacks from all sides. Country villages are awash with superstition, which has seriously overflowed into the churches. In the cities there are secular influences, such as the pursuit of money. How Christianity is to maintain the purity of its faith in the midst of this complex society is one of the tasks of theological reconstruction.[70]

Bishop Ting exhorts:

> Theological reconstruction is a safeguard to basic Christian faith, and it in no way attacks or changes it. Through theological reconstruction, our faith will gain a fairer and more reasonable exposition, thereby enabling believers to have a better and more confident understanding of their basic faith and enabling friends outside the church to be more receptive to the gospel message the church has for people.[71]

Rev. Cao Sheng-jie, the new general secretary of the China Christian Council, writes, "The Bible is inspired by God, the highest authority of faith. Our faith, based on the tenets of the Apostles Creed and the Nicene Creed, will never change." She continues, "Our theological thinking will be based on biblical teaching, historical church tradition, and our unique experience of the church and our culture.

[70] Yan, "What is Theology?" 37.

[71] K. H. Ting, "Adjustment of Theological Thinking is Unavoidable and Inevitable," *Tian Feng* 4 (2000): 4.

We hope our efforts will help in the all-around building of our church and make some contribution to the church universal."[72]

Missiological

For thirty years or more, the Chinese Communist Party neither thought nor spoke positively about the western missionary movement. In fact, it saw missionary endeavors closely linked to the opium trade carried out mostly by the British. Therefore, to them the sinicization of Christianity was of utmost importance.

During the past two hundred years, China had to accept numerous humiliations forced upon her by foreign governments. Events like the opium war, the arrow war, and the "unequal treaties" caused China to be bitter toward foreigners. In the wake of foreign advances into China, mission organizations used such leverage to spread the gospel. This caused the Chinese to resist even the work of well-meaning missionaries.

Sowing Seeds

Most of the early missionaries did not at first recognize the reason behind such Chinese hostility. They had come in obedience to the Lord, who had said, "Go, and make disciples of all nations." The vast majority of missionaries came to China with a deep conviction of God's mandate and call. They had been motivated by the love of Jesus to serve in China. Even though the communist government in the past tried for decades to degrade the work of missionaries, today many acknowledge once more the true and loving motives of those

---

[72] Rev. Cao Sheng-jie, *Chinese Theological Review* 16 (2002): 60–61. In an e-mail on April 12th 2005 to the author, Rev. Cao slightly modified her quote from the original publication which now reads: We believe that the Bible is the revelation from God.

missionaries. Today the younger generation and the young leaders of the church understand this.[73]

Once a young pastor pointed to hundreds of worshipers outside the church who had not been able to get seats inside the church, and said, "This is the fruit of your parents and other missionaries who labored here seventy years ago." They and countless other missionaries sowed the seed, but our Chinese brothers and sisters who faithfully followed in their footsteps now reap the harvest. God used both groups to build the body of Christ in that land. Chinese Christian leaders, following the principles of self-government, self-support and self-propagation, which they embraced fully, have seen phenomenal church growth in their country. No doubt they went out, being led by the Holy Spirit, and the Lord worked with them.

We have to embrace criticisms voiced by our Chinese friends, however, such as expressed by a professor in one of China's theological seminaries. He writes:

> The masses of church people seem to have an extremely shallow view of Christianity and thus are susceptible to cults and false teachings. What a number of Chinese scholars lament is that the Chinese church at the crucial junctures of history, at times of devastation for the nation and the people, have never of their own initiative played the just and moral role they should have taken. Western missionary evangelism in China was marked by exhorting Chinese people to abandon the Chinese cultural tradition, and thus the Chinese church, which has been deeply influenced by Western missionary preaching and devotional writing, has never really reflected theologically on its own ideas of evangelism.[74]

This, of course, in its totality is not quite accurate. Both western and Chinese writers, teachers, scholars, and missionaries have left a

---

[73] Also see the chapter on Bridging the Gulf Between Christians in China.
[74] Wang, "Theological Reconstruction," 21.

deep imprint on the lives of church people across China. We have to acknowledge the deep hurt some of our Chinese counterparts feel as they try to evaluate the history of their own people, however.

Fulfilling the Great Commission

One important matter that seems to be missing in the curriculum of China's theological education must be addressed. Western observers ask whether the Chinese church, with its absolute focus on reaching their own people, also has a vision or a strategy to fulfill Christ's mandate for world evangelization. Is this being taught? At a symposium sponsored by China Partner in conjunction with CCC, this question was put forward but not adequately answered. The Great Commission has been given to the universal church, and thus no church is exempt.

The unregistered church has reintroduced the Back to Jerusalem movement that at its core has a call to missions to other nations. As stated in a previous chapter, however, it has its flaws and needs a tremendous amount of guidance and prayer.

In the beginning of the twenty-first century God permits us to see what our forefathers—especially those who served as missionaries in China—were not privileged to see. God is doing a mighty work of grace in the most populous country of the world. Before Christianity was seen as an alien religion that tried to enter China on the coattails of enterprising western nations, but now it is accepted as a moral driving force that may counterattack the corruption and cynicism that spreads like cancer throughout China. But what are some of the areas in which we as westerners can get involved in a meaningful way without infringing on their rights to the Three-Self Principles? We can contribute to theological education from an evangelical perspective, such as offering seminars on evangelical and liberal theology in conjunction with our counterparts in China; symposiums between conservative and progressive theologians; lectures on various theological trends today; funding of evangelical scholarly works; and exchange of professors of theology, just to mention a few.

The German theologian and scholar Dr. Gotthard Oblau, who with his wife lived and worked in China for twelve years (in the 1980s and 90s), writes:

> Many of China's non-Christian intellectuals are interested today in a modern, enlightened Christianity such as they find in the West. Countless philosophers, historians and religious scholars, who research and teach in China's state-run institutes, study Christian thinking in the hope of finding in it something to enrich China's spiritual life and provide a moral and spiritual counterbalance to the crude and spiritless materialism which is spreading throughout the land at this current time.
>
> Theologians such as Bishop Ting find it highly regrettable that the same intellectuals, despite their spiritual interest in Christianity, hardly find any access to the Protestant Chinese church, which due to its style and appearance does not appeal to them. Also, the young theologians who have grown out of China's seminary education so far do not seem to be up to true intellectual dialogue with these circles.
>
> These are all justifiable concerns. Indeed, I believe we are talking here of a decisive theological dilemma which affects the future of the Chinese church.[75]

But there is hope! God is on the move. He is using His people in China as light posts across the entire nation. Theological education is playing and will continue to play a vital role in equipping emerging young Christian leaders for the enormous task to reach the yet unreached one billion plus Chinese. We in the West can learn much from what is transpiring in China—the land of my birth and the land I love.

---

[75] Oblau, "Theology Needs Freedom."

CHAPTER 11

Bridging the Gulf between Christians in China

The divisions of the body of Christ in China challenged me to always identify with the entire, true body of Christ and then to serve those belonging to it. Since 1981, when I began to visit China on a regular basis, I endeavored to understand the political situation to find the right perspective, and to look at the all-inclusive body of Christ.

On my first trip to China I stopped in Hong Kong to meet with so-called China specialists and China watchers. I took their advice seriously to be on guard against the "wolves in sheep's clothing." They warned me against contacting Christians associated with the "Three-Self-Patriotic Movement" (TSPM). They encouraged me to meet with leaders of house churches. I planned my trip accordingly.

I had difficulty finding house churches in China's interior. When I finally found one in a large city, I met with its leader. His dedication to Christ impressed me. The Christians associated with him seemed genuine. One of those believers led me to a newly opened registered church and left me there. He refused to attend the church service with me because he did not want to worship God with those believers. This startled me! I witnessed a large number of believers gathered together, united in their faith. The obvious reverence for God and love for the Scriptures overwhelmed me.

After this experience, I vowed not to seek one group of believers above another. I would seek fellowship with all those who belong to the true body of Christ. It no longer mattered to me whether believers worshiped in registered or unregistered churches. But I became painfully aware of the deep gulf between those two groups, and it was difficult at first to understand the reasons for such a division. The more I tried to discover the reasons, the stronger my desire grew to maintain fellowship with all believers of the body of Christ. Building bridges became my watchword because filling trenches was almost impossible to achieve. As time went by, my longing grew ever deeper to fellowship with all kinds of believers in China and to steer away from the counsel of overseas Christians who had encouraged me to fellowship with only one group—their group. Doing so, I believed, I would have a genuine opportunity to help build the kingdom of God on earth.

Abiding By The Law

Then I faced a dilemma. In order to work with unregistered churches, I would have to work in secrecy. This was contrary to my convictions. I wish to avoid judging those who have chosen to take that route, however.

Why was I hesitant to work in secrecy? During the Cold War, as a young Youth for Christ evangelist in Germany, my colleague Gottfried Lauth and I had a radio broadcast *Die Stimme der Jugend* (The Voice of Youth). Our voices penetrated the Iron Curtain and were heard by many in those countries.

We were invited by Dr. Horak, President of the Baptist Union of Yugoslavia, to preach in churches across that country. In spite of many restrictions placed on Christians at that time, we were grateful for many ministry opportunities.

One morning Dr. Horak was deeply disturbed. "I just received word that a number of Christians were thrown into prison," he told us.

We were stunned because we had not sensed any persecution while traveling through the country. "What happened?" we inquired.

"Two German missionaries left tracts wherever they traveled. They call this tract bombing," he explained. "To pass out tracts is forbidden by law in our land. Not knowing who left those tracts in public places, the police confronted local Christians and imprisoned some of them. Those missionaries may have had good intentions, but they were unwise in how they did their work. . . . No doubt by now they are giving glowing reports of their missionary endeavors in their homeland while our people sit in jail."

Right then I vowed that I would never do anything illegal but would always work with local Christians and abide by the law of the land.

Before going into China on my first trip, I had a motto that has remained with me on all subsequent trips: "Lord, give me courage to do the unusual and the sensitivity to know when to stop."

From the beginning I desired to do everything openly, honestly, and legally. This led to work with the registered church, the churches of the China Christian Council (CCC). What a blessing it has become! I also told their leaders that I wanted to maintain further contact with leaders of unregistered churches since they also belong to the body of Christ, and that I would do nothing to hinder the development of the church in China.

A gulf had been fixed between those two groups, and I had to come to terms with that fact.

What caused this gulf? How could this gulf be bridged? Should outsiders be involved in helping our Chinese brothers and sisters in bridging this gulf? Or would religious and political authorities in China misinterpret this as interference from the outside? I did not think so, but it had to be done with understanding and spiritual sensitivity. Let's examine the historical and political background of the problem facing us today.

The Historical Background

The Chinese viewed Christianity as an alien religion because it was seen as foreign. My parents, who had been missionaries in China with the China Inland Mission, were called "foreign devils." Why did the Chinese see it that way?

Going through reports that were sent by missionaries in those troubling times, I was surprised to see how deep the feelings of the Chinese ran. They harbored an astounding hatred toward foreigners. These feelings were primarily aimed at the British, whom they saw as the drug runners of the nineteenth century. They had instigated the Opium War, forced the Unequal Treaties[76] on them, and behaved like oppressors. Missionaries who had nothing to do with the despicable drug trade also bore China's rage.

I unearthed the following reports from the archives of the *Schweizer Allianz Mission*[77] (Swiss Alliance Mission), which had been an associate group of the China Inland Mission before the Second World War.

[76] The Unequal Treaties were a series of treaties signed by China and foreign powers during the nineteenth and twentieth centuries. They were called "unequal" because in most cases China was forced to pay astronomical amounts of reparation following military defeats, open up ports, cede lands, and make various concessions to foreign "spheres of influence." Under the Treaty of Nanjing the following ports were opened for foreign trade: Guangzhou, Xiamen, Fuzhou, Ningbo, and Shanghai. Under another, Treaties of Tianjin, eleven more ports were opened to Western trade. They were ratified by the Emperor in the Beijing Convention in 1860 after the end of the war. http://sources.Encyclopedia.org/wiki/TreatyofNanjing.

[77] *Chinaboten,* The Swiss Alliance Mission (SAM) was formerly united with the German branch of the China Inland Mission, called *Allianz China Mission.* SAM, Wolfensbergerstrasse 47, 8410 Winterthur, Switzerland, winterthur@sam-ame.org.

Presently an anti-British movement is felt all across China. This feeling goes very deep, so deep that other countries are affected by it as well. British goods are burned, the largest British harbor Hong Kong has been boycotted for months. Some Christians connected to British missions distance themselves and establish independent churches.
"The time will come that the name of 'England' will be hated by all other countries," thus the Asian press states openly. "Never before has the propaganda against Britain been subtler, quieter, yet penetrating deep to the core of Asian people."

In February 1927 missionary Gasser reported:

Our old itinerant bookseller Chang returned home deeply depressed. For the second time he encountered soldiers who yanked Bibles and tracts out of his hands and threw them on the ground. They called him "slave of foreigners" and threatened to kill him. This is another indication how we have to minister under tough and dire conditions.
On a daily basis mass meetings are being held at a Confucian temple. Now their anger is directed against Britain. All British people should be expelled and all of their merchandise should be burned. They erected a stage. They displayed a person to represent the British. His hands were bound on his back and then they enumerated all of the sins the British commit. . . . My husband and I knelt together in the chapel and entrusted ourselves into the hands of the Lord. We need urgent prayers. My husband suffers under such a burden.
Posters are being used to defame the Christians: "Christians are dogs of imperialism"; "Leprous, drunken, and a miserable Christian crowd"; "Down with Jesus-people"; "Down with foreigners and Christianity."

Corruption caused by warlords, and later on by the nationalists, drove many Chinese into the arms of the communists during the 1920s and 1930s. Didn't communism promise equality for all Chinese, patriotism for their country, and the removal of all injustice? What noble goals! Even Christians fell under the spell of this new ideology. Christians with liberal theology were especially susceptible to these new ideas. They wanted to be part of the greater movement of those who dreamed of a new, stronger, and more glorious China!

Political Development After 1949

"The Chinese people have stood up,"[78] announced Mao Zedong on October 1, 1949, overlooking the Tiananmen Square. China would belong entirely to the Chinese. China alone would determine how she would live. The government asked all foreigners to leave the country. Before doing so, all foreign companies and mission organizations had to undergo strict investigations and inspections by the new rulers. Everyone had to provide evidence that they had not mistreated the Chinese during their stay in China, and only then were they allowed to leave the country. My parents were finally released in 1950.

To oversee matters of the Protestant church in China, the government established the institution "Three-Self Patriotic Movement." (TSPM). This was done in the early fifties. Everything and everybody in China had to submit to the will of the Party. Consequently all Christian churches were obliged to submit to this movement. Many of them did, others did not. Bible-believing and evangelical Christians, especially those from independent (nondenominational or non-confessional) churches, particularly those that had been started by Chinese, were reluctant to join the new and quasi-political structure. The government arrested a number of those church leaders, preachers, pastors, and evangelists and sentenced them to prison.

The TSPM, with the blessing of the Party, was subject to its political interpretation. Government policies could then be imposed

---

[78] Li Zhisui, *The Private Life Of Chairman Mao,* 52.

upon the churches. What is the meaning of Three-Self? It can be summarized by the following:

Self-Support—to be financially independent and forbidden to accept foreign support.

Self-Propagation—to proclaim the gospel only by the Chinese themselves and not with people from abroad.

Self-Governing—to independently lead and care for the church in China without depending upon foreign involvement.

According to the constitution of 1954, the People's Republic of China assured every citizen "liberty and religious freedom," as spelled out in Article 88. The reality, however, proved to be different. The oppression against Christians and other religious beliefs continued. It is illuminating what John Fraser wrote in his book *The Chinese*.

> Old habits are hard to break, and most objective observers, Chinese and foreign, feel that it will be a long time before there will be substantial changes, a criminal code notwithstanding. After all, China has long and eloquent constitutions guaranteeing freedom of speech and religion, neither of which exists. To allow people to openly express their political thoughts strikes at the roots of Communism, and so as old heresies are forgiven, new ones fill up the dungeons. It is not properly understood in the West that Communism is a secular religion, that to question the dictatorship of the proletariat is as unforgivable as questioning the doctrine of papal infallibility or transubstantiation in the Roman Catholic Church. In the West, the Church no longer has the temporal power to enforce its doctrine, but when it did its actions were not unlike those of the Party.[79]

The worst persecution of the communist era took place during the Cultural Revolution (1966–76). All churches were closed, the Bible was forbidden, and Christians could meet only secretly in small groups. Other religions were equally banned.

---

[79] Fraser, *The Chinese,* 387.

Throughout mission history in China, suffering was a key element in church life. On different occasions Christianity became extinct. For example, the Nestorians were muted in the ninth century and forced to close all monasteries and to halt all missionary activities. Again in the fourteenth century the Franciscans experienced the same fate. After the communists took power in 1949 (in China this is referred to as "liberation"), and particularly during the Cultural Revolution, continuous persecution was severe, which included imprisonment, exile, labor camps, and sometimes death. This period of suffering and the succeeding resurrection of the Chinese church can be seen in five different periods.* Followers of other religions besides Christianity suffered as well. Here, however, we will focus on the plight of Christians.

1. The Body of Christ during Oppression (1949–58)

After "liberation" the government tried to completely subjugate the churches under state rule. In the early years of communist rule, their goal was to prevent all contact between Christians in China and their foreign "mother churches." Foreign missionaries were expelled, and those who tried to remain in the country were charged during "struggle meetings" and often sentenced. At times, Chinese Christians were executed. Many institutions operated by Christians, such as mission schools, hospitals, orphanages, schools for the blind, and church buildings, were closed or taken over by the party or municipal governments.

2. The Body of Christ during Times of Hardship (1958–66)

During this period the communist government eased its persecution of the church. Christians were allowed to practice their faith with more freedom. The party increased its pressure against churches to rid themselves totally of all foreign influences, however. They desired to purify the church from any remaining foreign influence and "capitalistic imperialism." During this period the split between believers and the churches reached its peak—one group led by the TSPM, and the other by leaders of non-registered churches. The latter were seen as illegal and thus were persecuted.

3. The Body of Christ Threatened by Extinction (1966–76)

During this decade, also called "the lost generation," the Cultural Revolution brought turmoil to the entire country. Hundreds of thousands (possibly even millions) of people died, and a number of those victims were Christians. Persecution forced all Christians underground in order to survive. Christians lived out their faith only within the confines of their immediate family.

4. The Period of Slow Awakening of the Body of Christ (1976–79)

After Zhou Enlai and Mao Zedong had died in 1976, some of the government policies were changed. Government leaders realized how dependent they were upon the know-how and investments of industrialized Western powers. Furthermore, they needed to become true partners of the world community. This, of course, alleviated the pressure on all religious communities. In 1979, the first church was opened in Ningbo (Zhejiang), then in Shanghai, then Beijing, and other cities followed rapidly.

5. The Body of Christ in the New China (1979 to present)

Presently about 20 million Christians worship freely in over 17,000 church buildings and at least 35,000 registered house churches, also called meeting points. Millions more assemble in unregistered house churches. Christians who meet in churches and meeting points affiliated with the CCC can easily be counted, and their numbers can be substantiated. This is not the case with those who meet in unregistered house churches.

The CCC, which oversees and regulates the interests of registered churches, was established in the early 1980s and has since proven to be a binding force among churches. The council is in close contact with foreign denominations and Christian organizations. Unfortunately, many overseas evangelical leaders are still reluctant to cooperate, fellowship with, and befriend believers within the churches of the CCC.

I deeply regret that the gulf between Chinese believers, initially caused by political developments in China, has not been overcome because of attitudes among a number of evangelicals overseas. In China efforts are being made to find ways of rapprochement; overseas efforts are rare and proceed very cautiously at best. In a number of regions in China, house churches have now registered with the government and thus found fellowship with the CCC. More and more house churches are following suit. The spirit of reconciliation, extended more readily by members of the CCC, is finally bearing fruit.

Dr. Kleiner, a former missionary to Africa with the Swiss Alliance Mission, traveled to China with a China Partner teaching team and reported:

> The China Christian Council has been and still is ostracized by many evangelicals in the West. The reasons are because the CCC is supposedly controlled by the communist government and/or she has contact with the World Council of Churches. Some even say that leaders of the CCC have learned the vocabulary of evangelical Christians in order to delude evangelical visitors from overseas. The truth, however, (so say the critics) is that they are not Christians at all, but they are only pretending. In my opinion, it is unjustified and tragic to avoid Christians within the CCC, because by doing so it affects and hurts the entire body of Christ worldwide. It deprives evangelicals of the possibility to share in the awakening and in the spiritual life that is taking place within the CCC. By doing

> so, it only leads and encourages members of the CCC to move to a closer contact with theologically liberal churches in the West. The general notion that leaders of the CCC are not Christians at all is very painful to them and to us as well who fellowship with those believers. . . . According to my experience it is wrong to say that Christians of the CCC are spiritually cold, liberal, or dead. To the contrary, we encountered dynamic spiritual life.

This is exactly what I have experienced on all my trips to China. Of course, like everything else in life, there are exceptions. By far most of the Christians in China, who belong to CCC churches, are Bible believing, Christ-centered, and evangelical.

Why The Tensions Between The Two Groups?

Tensions exist between church leaders of the CCC and leaders of various groups within the house church movement. Even today many leaders of house churches refuse to fellowship with those who belong to CCC churches, and they refuse to register their churches with the authorities. On the other hand, positive developments have taken place in that members of both groups are finding each other. In the past, registrations had to be made with the TSPM. Several years ago this regulation changed so that house churches can register directly with municipal authorities.

A dear brother, who is an elder in one of the CCC churches in Shanghai, regrets this division. He believes house church leaders do not want to unite with the CCC for three main reasons:

1. In the early days (before the Cultural Revolution) some of the leaders of the TSPM collaborated[80] with the communist regime.
2. Leaders of house churches act rather independently and thus are responsible to no one. In order to keep their position of power within their respective groups, they continue to foster resentment against the CCC and its leadership and thus foster enmity.
3. Christians who years ago fled China cannot forget the reason for having done so. Now, having the opportunity to visit their former homeland, they sow seeds of division and stir up distrust against the CCC.

No doubt leaders within house churches have a deep desire to live out their faith in total freedom and to spread the gospel throughout their country. On the other hand, and unfortunately so, large segments within the house church movement have distanced themselves from biblical foundations and propagate heretical teachings. Some of them have become cults and mix their beliefs with those of folk religions. This is a sore spot often mentioned by leaders of the CCC. Christian leaders in China have told me that some of the heresies are home grown while others have been imported from overseas.

Interestingly, Bishop Ting, in a letter dated September 28, 1988, wrote a stern rebuke to the authorities of the Guangdong province.

---

[80] There is a difference between collaboration and cooperation. To collaborate means to be in tune with one particular group and its ideology and agenda. To collaborate with the Communist Party means that you believe in its ideology and help its leaders to disseminate its beliefs and values. To cooperate means to go along with their rules, regulations, and laws as long as they do not challenge your faith. Let me give you a simple example. To travel to China or to do business there, you have to work with the government's foreign affairs department to receive a visa. The government then gives you the right and privilege to see the sights, study, or work in China as long as you abide by the laws of the land, but it does not force you to push its ideological agenda. You cooperate with them as you abide by their rules, regulations, or laws, but you do not collaborate with them.

He took a strong stand defending the rights of unregistered house churches. Even though this is quite outdated, it still shows the struggles that took place within China's society as they tried to develop rights for Christians within its borders.

A foreign observer mentioned three reasons he feels are put forth by those who refuse to register:

1. Political—rejection of communism.
2. Historical—denunciation of non-registered churches by those who belong to the TSPM, especially in the period before the Cultural Revolution.
3. Theological—rejection of liberal theology found within sections of the TSPM; rigidity in believing that their faith (house church) alone is the correct one and therefore they rigorously refuse to work with other churches and Christians.

In order to understand the reasons for the gulf that now exists between the two groups, and the ones that brought it about, we must explore the background that led to the split during the period of communist rule. Christianity in China had to prove itself over a period of decades. Let me mention five different aspects:

1. *Political*—as mentioned earlier, China has always been a patriotic (nationalistic) country. She considered herself to be the center of the world. Today you can still visit a spot in Beijing, which, according to the Chinese, is seen as the "center of the world." Did missionaries have enough sensitivity to really understand this political issue?
2. *Cultural*—China is the country with the oldest culture. Throughout the centuries, civilizations cultivated in China and great teachers determined the development of the country. The best known and most esteemed of those was the sage Confucius (551–479 BC), whose teachings during the past two millennia became the backbone of Chinese civilization.

How did the missionaries confront these well-established ethical teachings with its *Weltanschauung*?

3. *Religious*—religions such as Buddhism and Taoism have existed in China for a long period of time, and they viewed Christianity as a danger. Did missionaries have to meet head-on with proponents of these religions and study their teachings? Of course. The question is how did they confront those well-rooted religions?
4. *Historical*—different types of mission organizations worked in China. Some belonged to liberal organizations, others belonged to evangelical groups. Later Chinese Christians established their own mission organizations and often did not like to cooperate with their foreign counterparts. When the TSPM was established, it enhanced the split between the leadership of registered and non-registered churches.
5. *Human*—as found in countries the world over, differences of opinion exist regarding interpretation of the Bible and the perception of Christian beliefs. Watchman Nee, for example, was exclusive in his stance and had difficulty working with foreigners. He even had problems working with Chinese Christians who were under the jurisdiction of foreign mission boards. Even though he had this weakness, his writings were greatly appreciated by Christians around the world. But behavior like this resulted in unspiritual and carnal mindsets, which, of course, hindered the unity of Christians.

Finding Solutions

How can foreigners build bridges, or better yet, help to bridge the gulf between Chinese believers? Let me mention three areas:

Avoid the Negatives

Foreigners should avoid what could be seen as negative and interpreted as such, which easily results in negative thinking. For example:

1. Do not make unsubstantiated claims as to how many Christians live in China today. No one knows!
2. Do not criticize leading Christians, no matter what group they belong to in China.
3. Don't make false declarations about persecuted Christians in China, such as "60 million Christians in China are brutally persecuted today," as was stated in an evangelical video. Who has actually counted those 60 million? Or on the other hand, why do so many suppress the fact that there are at least 20 million Christians (2004) who freely assemble to worship God and live out their faith without fear?
4. Don't declare that persecution of Christians is a planned policy of China's government. It is not! As someone said, "What bleeds, reads." Everybody knows that bad news travels faster than good news, and some relish in propagating bad news. The son of a highly respected church leader in the United States told me once, "It is a shame that Christians overseas have lowered themselves to raising funds on the back of formerly persecuted Chinese Christians."

Highlight the Positives

Foreigners should be willing to highlight the positive development of the body of Christ in China. It is important to mention the positive side of what is happening in China, which will encourage our fellow believers. I want to caution against exaggerating the positive developments, however. We must be fair and balanced in our reporting. The positive side needs to be reported. We can rejoice in numerous advancements.

We can be grateful for the improvement in China in areas of economics and culture; for the resurrection of the church after the terrible period of the Cultural Revolution; for the growth of the church in China, which is estimated to have a constituency of millions; for opportunities in some parts of China to resume youth and Sunday School work; for the majority of Christians in China who are Bible-believing and evangelical; for the great interest shown in the gospel by university students and intellectuals; for over 42 million Bibles and New Testaments that have been printed since the Cultural Revolution (2004 statistics); for theological seminaries and Bible schools that operate in twenty-three cities across China where close to 2,000 students are being trained for the Lord's work; for up to 50,000 churches that have opened since the Cultural Revolution; for Christians in China who are actively engaged in humanitarian efforts; for the improved relationship between house churches and the CCC in many areas; and for the CCC's effort to cooperate with evangelicals abroad.

One of my great concerns is that many churches lack well-trained pastors and church workers. Only a few overseas theological schools give scholarships to students from China, however. Furthermore, the situation in China is often reported by evangelicals in a biased and unbalanced fashion, perpetuating horror stories of the past.

Fellowship with All Believers Across China

Evangelicals from overseas have gravitated to believers of unregistered house churches and tried to help them. This is good and should be done in the future—but openly, legally, and honestly as done by a number of evangelical groups. Evangelicals should also be willing to fellowship with Christians of the CCC and strengthen them with prayers and support. The vast majority of CCC church members—like the unregistered Christians—are true believers who love the Lord Jesus and with whom we can have wonderful fellowship in the gospel. As for those who live as nominal Christians, friendly relationships should be maintained, so that they also may sense our desire to lift up Jesus who wants to be Lord of all.

Much has changed for the positive in China, and we thank God for the phenomenal church growth in that land. Even though gulfs remain that separate Christians, we rejoice with those who have bridged the gulf and found each other. I pray that we in foreign countries help build those bridges. Let us pray with Jesus, "That they may all be one; as thou, Father, art in me, and I in thee, that they also may be one in us: that the world may believe that thou hast sent me" (John 17:21, KJV).

*Some information gleaned from "Religion und Christentum in der Volksrepublik China", Eicholz Brief 3/87, Hgb. G. Rüther & K. Weigelt.

Chapter 12

Theological Reconstruction—Necessity and Danger

Across the lunch table sat one of our close pastor friends in China. "What do you think about the attempt of some of our Chinese church leadership to reconstruct theological thinking?" he asked.

I had heard about this reconstruction concept but needed to find out in depth what this was all about. "Do you mean that the theology of the Christian church will receive a new meaning here in China? Will it differ from biblical truths that have come down the ages to our day?" I inquired.

"Not really," he answered, "but for instance, some of our theologians are talking about diluting the doctrine of justification by faith."

"Diluting what!" I gasped. "This is one of the cornerstones of our evangelical faith."

New Revelation?

"Yes, it should remain so," he replied, "but isn't it true that from time to time new spiritual discoveries have changed theological thinking? Diluting may be the wrong word. Some call it 'fading out' (*danhua*) or deemphasizing. What they mean is to refocus on other biblical truths rather than to keep focusing simply on one, like justification by faith."

"What do you mean?" I knew that Bible principles are transcultural. In order to understand such principles, however, hermeneutics[81] must be applied.

"Remember, how the apostle Peter received a new, dramatic revelation?" he continued. "While praying on the housetop, he had a vision of a sheet with many types of animals being let down from heaven. The Lord told him to kill and eat—but Peter initially refused because of their strict dietary laws. This revelation that God had cleansed what Peter had formerly considered unclean forced the early Jewish believers to embrace all people. God intended the gospel to reach the world and not just His chosen people.[82] The heathen suddenly became the focus of evangelism; they now had the same right as the Jews to become followers of Jesus. Then the apostle Paul taught that circumcision was no longer necessary for believers."

"Later Martin Luther reintroduced the doctrine of justification by faith as taught by the apostle Paul in his letters to the Romans and Galatians. This upset the Roman Catholic Church and the church's teaching of that day. This even split the church. The Protestant Lutheran church was born. Years later the Baptists had their biblical convictions and split from the Lutherans. Then the Mennonites emphasized their teachings on pacifism."

"All that is true, and I understand," I argued, "but it sounds strange or even suspect when the term reconstruction is being used. We do not dare reconstruct biblical teaching."

A distinction must be made between new revelations received during the period of Acts (e.g. the apostle Peter in the house of Cornelius) when Scripture was still being written, and later when Scripture was

---

[81] The study of the principles of interpretation—both the grammatico-historical interpretation and the practical application of that interpretation in the pulpit—is called hermeneutics. Walter A. Elwell, ed., *Evangelical Dictionary of Theology* (Grand Rapids, Michigan: 1984), 565.

[82] Acts 10:34–35; 15:6–17; 10:24–48. See also Romans 3:29–30; 9:24; 10:12–13.

canonized. Some still ask: Is Scripture closed, or is God still revealing new truth? If it is not closed, then we open ourselves to all sorts of experientially-based understandings on par with the Bible.

New Challenges

"Our theologians don't want to change what the Bible teaches, but they want to receive new insights that will help the church in China find its own identity," he explained. "For too long our Christian believers have been marginalized by our fellow citizens. We must find a way to reach their hearts, so that not only the common, mostly uneducated people of our land will find Jesus, but also the intellectuals. A battle for the mind of the Chinese is taking place, and we need to win that battle."

His approach intrigued me. Even more, it demonstrated some of the Chinese Christian leaders' passion to reach those who have no idea what Christianity is all about. In order to win China for Christ, theological thinking has to be advanced. This, however, should be done by encouraging our Chinese counterparts to use proper hermeneutics. An extremely interesting development is presently taking place in the Chinese church; nevertheless, many believers inside and outside of China have been deeply disturbed. I personally believe the word reconstruction should not have been used. Reconstruction in English has a different connotation and is misleading. It is unfortunate that this term was chosen.

Pan Naizhao, a Hong Kong Chinese, wrote:

> Since theological reconstruction in China was formally launched at the Jinan Conference, it has attracted heated discussion within and outside of China. In particular, the proposal "Fading out the doctrine of Justification by Faith" was a cause of grave concern, especially among Protestants. Some would even challenge whether

> the Church of China has abandoned the Christian faith; or, indeed, whether it has reverted to a liberal theological position.[83]

An added dimension comes into play, however, which needs to be considered. The Chinese government wants to get all religious and nonreligious groups on the same page with their unswerving ideology of socialism. To them this means socialism with Chinese characteristics. These characteristics now also spell capitalism. No other communistic state has embraced capitalism, but China has. Its leaders now recognize a new aspect, that of a communistic/capitalistic society.

How does the church face up to this challenge? How will "socialism with capitalistic overtones" affect the church? Can the church wholeheartedly accept this type of socialism or even adapt its teachings to go along with theirs? Here again they need to apply biblical principles to specific aspects of Chinese society.

We need to pay close attention to these important developments. Chinese Christians are our brothers and sisters—they are part of the worldwide body of believers. What happens there will affect us, and vice versa. We dare not sit on the sidelines. On the other hand, we dare not meddle. They have the same rights to develop their own biblical and theological thinking, as we do in South America, Africa, Europe, and in North America. But deferential dialogue is good and necessary.

Above all, the Bible, as the fully inspired Word of God, must remain the underpinning and the basis of all truth.

Progressive Thinking In The West

Theological thinking is also being challenged in the West. I just read an article in *Christianity Today* (CT) "The Emergent Mystique"

---

[83] *Nanjing Theological Review,* no. 57 (December 2003): 157–58.

in which Brian McLaren, a pastor and the author of the book *A New Kind of Christian*, articulates a new biblical understanding on how to reach nonbelievers for Christ. CT writes:

> . . . he (McLaren) has questions about other cherished words in the evangelical vocabulary.
> "I don't think we've got the gospel right yet. What does it mean to be 'saved'? When I read the Bible, I don't see it meaning, 'I'm going to heaven after I die.' Before modern evangelism nobody accepted Jesus Christ as their personal Savior, or walked down an aisle, or said the sinner's prayer."
> It's not that McLaren is interested in joining the liberal side of modern Protestantism. "I don't think the liberals have it right. But I don't think we have it right either. None of us has arrived at orthodoxy."
> Comments like these make many evangelicals nervous.[84]

Efforts to rethink the way to win nonbelievers for Christ, like the ones McLaren propounds, are now accepted by a number of younger and more progressive pastors. Theological thinking has become important to them. How does this relate to the efforts of our Chinese counterparts? Let's see.

Christianity Today continues to dissect this phenomenon:

> If critics overlook the evangelistic energy of the emerging church, they also often lump together two very different kinds of postmodern thought. The most notorious postmodern thinkers have been the "deconstructionists"—French intellectuals like Jacques Derrida and Michel Foucault who seek to show that the cherished ideas of Western society (and Christian faith) are fatally compromised by internal contradictions.

[84] "The Emergent Mystique," *Christianity Today* 48, no. 11 (November 2004), 36.

Thus we see a definite trend as Western theologians—and even pastors of newly formed and emerging churches—reexamine theological thinking. In order to grapple with some of these issues, I will examine the convictions of some other Western theologians as they question the emergence of theological thinking even though they may have slightly different interpretations as to what is going on in the theological world in China.

Since the word *reconstruction* became confusing and controversial to some, the word *construction* is now also being used. But the move to realign theological thinking remains the same, no matter what terms are being used.

A Raging Controversy

One of our China Partner board members had something to say about the raging controversy surrounding the Chinese church's desire to find its own understanding and view of theological thinking. Dr. Ralph Covell, senior professor at Denver Theological Seminary, wrote the following editorial: [85]

> Five years ago, the China Christian Council (CCC) met in Jinan [Shandong province] and adopted a resolution to launch theological construction in China. Since then, theological construction has attracted worldwide attention. However, many people don't really understand its background and goals. Some are worried that theological construction is unbiblical and will change the basic doctrines of the Christian faith in China. Theological construction was not launched to alter the Christian faith; its basic purpose is to pave the way for more effective gospel ministry.
>
> Nearly all of the churches in China belonging to the CCC are very conservative in their Christian beliefs. Because of this many

[85] Dr. Ralph Covell, "Reconstructing Theological Thinking," *CHINA NEWS* 11, no. 2 (Spring 2004), 1.

believers interpret certain Scripture in extreme ways. They believe, for example, that a verse like 2 Corinthians 6:14, "Do not be unequally yoked with unbelievers," means that they should have no relationships with non-Christian people. The world, in their thinking, is only filled with evil, sin, and unrighteousness. To avoid having any link with unbelievers causes them to refuse to collaborate with them in projects of social welfare, community development, and nation building. In some cases they feel it is wrong to shake hands with unbelievers or to have friendly relationships with them even in church. Because of the prevalence of such attitudes, national leaders of the CCC have proposed the need to rethink certain biblical truths.

The first issue would be what is the relationship between believers and unbelievers? Does the biblical truth, justification by faith, for example, lead to the conclusion that believers can have no relationship with unbelievers? Would it not be better perhaps for preachers to emphasize less the idea that "those who believe in Jesus go to heaven and those who refuse Him to hell"? Apart from a few, there seem to be none who are denying the spiritual difference between those who are "saved" and "unsaved." Rather they suggest that in the socialist environment of current China it would be better to preach much more on the love of God and His care for all of creation.

In the view of these leaders, certain biblical truths need to take precedence[86] over other truths when God's people face differing situations. They justify this by showing how the Bible records differing attitudes that early Christians took to the state. In Romans 13:16, Paul urges believers to be "subject to governing authorities," since the authorities reigned "in righteousness" and ruled "with justice." However, conditions changed in the Roman world, and the state became wicked and tyrannical. Therefore, when John wrote Revelation, believers were no longer to submit to the state, but to oppose it. Conditions had changed, and there was a need to rethink biblical teaching on the state.

---

[86] I would prefer using the word *emphasis* rather than *precedence*.

> In the process of rethinking biblical truth, the emphasis during the last five years has been on the relationship between believers and nonbelievers. At the present time another topic is being discussed—the Christian's view of the Bible. What is actually meant by saying that "the Bible is the Word of God"? Have believers exalted the Bible to the position that it is, as it were, the fourth member of the Trinity with a certain magical quality? Is every word actually God's truth or are there portions which, although authorized by God, are yet only human opinions? K. H. Ting, president of Union Theological Seminary in Nanjing, the largest seminary in China, has pointed, for example, to the false opinions of Job's comforters which obviously are not God's truth. This approach to rethinking one's view of the Bible has made many Chinese Christians nervous. They fear that such restructuring of people's thinking could lead to the denial, not merely the rethinking, of Bible truth. Bishop Ting emphasizes that the central truth of the Bible as God's Word is that "God is love," and that this is the message to be proclaimed in China.
>
> As the church in China is going through this period of "restructuring theological thinking," let us join with them in prayer and conversation that they may be helped in preparing the church to be an effective witness of God's love and truth to all the peoples of that great country.

Dr. Covell mentioned the matter of believers versus unbelievers. No one denies that all Christian believers must have normal relationships with nonbelievers. The debate goes deeper than this, however. In order to reach out to nonbelievers some of the Chinese Christian leaders also feel that through God's all-encompassing love, all human beings will eventually be accepted by Him. Justification by love supersedes justification by faith. This, of course, cannot be backed up by Scripture. Love alone is inadequate by itself to describe God. In its ultimate conclusion this leads to universalism. Both love and holiness are appropriate biblical descriptions and should never be separated.

It must be noted, however, that Bishop Ting never used the term "justification by love." When asked about this term, he answered, "Justification by love is a poor and misleading imitation of justification by faith. I have never approved of its usage. It can cause a lot of confusion and is not conducive to clear definition of terms."[87]

On this subject Tobias Brandner of Hong Kong said the following:

> It is striking how "love" assumes an important significance in the Chinese churches. I can't think of any church I have visited which hadn't a poster of the Chinese character of "love" hanging in a prominent position. K. H. Ting speaks for the whole of the Chinese church when he says: "The root attribute of God is not His omnipotence, or His omniscience, or His omnipresence, or His self-existence, or His majesty and glory, but His love."[88]

It is not so much the words *reconstruction* or *construction* that concerns me, because I also believe that Chinese Christians need to find how to best reach their countrymen whether those two words are being used or not. It is a noble cause to advance correct theological thinking, and our Chinese friends are wrestling with these issues now. We should encourage them in this endeavor. In order to do so, however, believers—and I mean all believers everywhere—must study Scripture and get their marching orders from that book and not from us in the western world. Let me repeat, hermeneutics must be done to find the right path in their quest to establish theology with "Chinese characteristics." For example, it may lead them to evangelize differently than we do in the West. It may not be radio or TV evangelism, nor may it be tract distribution or street preaching.

---

[87] Bishop K. H. Ting, *God is Love* (Colorado Springs, CO: Cook Communications Ministries International, 2004), 621.

[88] *Nanjing Theological Review,* no. 57, December 2003.

Most registered and unregistered church members in China have done something very well. They have lived not so much as Christians but as followers of Jesus. Their lifestyle has attracted nonbelievers to Christ. They try to emulate the apostle Paul who said, "Be ye followers of me, even as I also am of Christ."[89] Passing out tracts is not a bad idea, wherever this can be done. But being *living tracts*[90] is far more convincing to nonbelievers. It is tough to follow the example of Paul, but many Chinese Christians seem to take this seriously.

Other Perspectives

What do others say about the reconstruction issue? Rev. Peter K. H. Lee,[91] a Hong Kong theologian, wrote an article, "What has the Chinese Church's 'Theological Reconstruction' to do with us?" He first puts forth a statement from Elder Ji, President of China's Three-Self Patriotic Movement:

> Theological construction is what preachers, believers, and the church seek to explicate, directly and systematically, the object and content of beliefs. Theological construction is not the same as "basic beliefs." Basic beliefs refer to the object and content of basic Christian beliefs as summarized in the Apostles' Creed and the Nicene Creed.

Rev. Lee then continues:

> Hong Kong being separated from mainland China by just a thin line, we in Hong Kong can see clearly the church situations across the border and can understand with no difficulty the urgent need for sound theological education and theological construction.

---

[89] 1 Cor. 11:1, KJV.

[90] The apostle Paul touches on this in 2 Corinthians 3.

[91] Professor of Theology and Culture at the Lutheran Theological Seminary, Hong Kong.

He points out that with the introduction of Christianity to China, western missionaries delivered "denominational distinctions and theological disputes." Also "quarrels between fundamentalism and liberalism and tension between evangelicalism and ecumenism" have left scars to this day.

For these reasons alone, he believes that theological thinking must be challenged and attempts undertaken to let theological construction or reconstruction take its course. This is necessary both in China and Hong Kong. He writes:

> Socialists speak of humanistic civilization. Confucians dwell on benevolence, righteousness, and morality. Liberals advocate freedom and human rights. They all have some things of value to offer, yet they all fall short of a perfect blueprint for an ideal society. If we turn to Christian thought, we can find in the Bible invaluable teachings on the nature of humanity. The Bible teaches that humans are created in the image of God, which means that they are endowed with dignity and worth to begin with. But humans have fallen, marring the divine image in them. They can be restored to their dignity and worth through the redemptive work of Christ, and, further, they can develop their potential more fully as exemplified by Christ, as fully God and fully human.
>
> This need not be merely a dogma but can be witnessed to by the followers of Christ and the Church's ministry. Call this theology, if you will, but it can be lived, it has something substantial to say, and can stimulate dialogue with socialists [as espoused in China], Confucians, and liberal social thinkers in their common quest for human worth.

Rev. Lee is convinced that some good can come forth by readdressing the topic of theological (re)construction. In his conclusion he writes:

> Now is the time for theological teachers and students, pastors and disciples of Christ to open up their hearts and minds to the inspiration of the Spirit, so that they can use proper and lively methods of hermeneutics to bring out living truths of the Bible. This is the basis of hope for churches in China and Hong Kong.[92]

No matter what challenges the Chinese church faces, it needs to rely on the Scriptures. The word of God is a plumbline for all workmen who endeavor to build on the foundation of Christ in any culture or country.

Thinking Critically

A much harder and more critical look is taken by Li Xinyuan, a Bible scholar and apologist living in the United States. He clearly states his displeasure with Bishop Ting's push to (re)construct theological thinking in China. In his book *Theological Construction—or Destruction*[93] he takes the bishop to task. He addresses Ting's Christology, his view of God, and his view on the "Cosmic Christ" among other pertinent subjects.

> Ding's[94] *Essays*[95] *[Love Never Ends]* are a combination of many different thoughts and perspectives.... He mixes together Marxist dialectical materialism, his own imaginary religious Communism, liberal theology, as well as his reinterpretation of the sociological perspectives of Wu Yaozong, and his subjective interpretations

---

[92] Peter K. H. Lee, "What has the Chinese Church's 'Theological Reconstruction' to do with us?" Message, no. 252, April 2003. Hong Kong Christian Council.

[93] Li Xinyuan, *Theological Construction—or Destruction* (Streamwood, IL: Christian Life Press, 2003).

[94] Some spell Bishop Ting's name with a D—Ding Guangxuan.

[95] *Essays* refer to the Bishop's book *Collected Essays,* which in the translated English version became *Love Never Ends.*

> of the theology of Teilhard de Chardin, process theology, and liberation theology. One can see the gradual process by which he formed his ecclesiology based on Three-Self and supported by the political power of the Party. In this mixture, some ideas were taken by him without any change while others were developed by him. Sometimes he uses de Chardin's words to say what he wants to say—at other times he lets Alfred North Whitehead speak for him. When he needs evidence to support his view of "the Cosmic Christ," Ding states that de Chardin had already talked about this idea. When Ding seeks to formulate his own view of God, he states that Whitehead's God fascinated him. Many passages in Ding's *Essays* cleverly use the ideas of other theologians and philosophers to express his own subtle meaning.
>
> Because the *Essays* do contain some elements of Christian faith, we cannot simply view them as only treatises on political or social theories. Yet, because they are filled with secular, political, and cultural perspectives, we cannot treat them simply as theology either. Ding's thought is merely the product of the politico-religious figure that emerged from a particular environment, for the purpose of "accommodating" God's word to human Communist "ideology." Ding's "accommodation" is heartfelt but thoroughly misleading because in actuality, Chinese Communism is his "basic belief" and "ultimate concern." In the *Essays*, Ding does not openly admit his belief in Communism, but he indirectly describes it as "the community of mankind according to God's will" or "a higher faith" (*Essays*, p. 213 and 109). Ding is clearly aware of his peculiar status. He can easily find his "position" on China's "socio-political map" (*Essays*, p. 108). In his *Essays* Ding strives to find a theological basis for his "basic belief"—which is basically Marxist.[96]

This interesting booklet is not so much an explanation of how to cope with the concept of theological (re)construction but rather a refutation of Ting's theology.

---

[96] Li Xinyuan, *Theological Construction—or Destruction*, 28–29.

One of the most scathing attacks on Ting's theological view on the "Cosmic Christ" and his social gospel is found in the chapter on Ting's Christology:

> Eckerton [a British pastor who was a member of the British Communist Party] once told Ding: "The Communist Party encouraged me to be a good pastor, while my religious belief demanded that I be a good Party member" (*Essays*, p. 508).
>
> I am not clear how Pastor Eckerton of England managed to merge Communist and Christian pastor in one person (a wisdom neither God nor man can undertake). But I know Mr. Ding's efforts in this regard have been remarkable. He can put his fundamental beliefs and the ideology of his political organization in the overall framework of Christian theological deliberation, thus merging the two systems so effectively that his fundamental beliefs have appeared to have gained a reasonable theological explanation, potentially endangering the biblical faith of the Chinese church. Yet simultaneously he wins praise and plaudits from both the deceived and his co-conspirators alike. This point becomes clear from the relationship between his Cosmic Christ and his concern for the present world system.[97]

Bishop Ting, no doubt, is the leading Chinese liberal theologian of our time. As the elder Christian spokesperson, however, he is highly revered by many mainland Chinese counterparts. Even though many Christian leaders within the CCC circles follow his directives, many others do not. The debate on this issue will go on.

Understanding Bishop Ting

When I first met Bishop Ting in 1984 at the airport of Bangalore, India, he warmly invited me to Nanjing, his home. Over the years

---

[97] Ibid., 65.

we have become good friends. He opened the way for us to teach in theological seminaries and Bible schools across China. We spent hours together discussing all aspects of the church situation in China. With his help I got a better understanding of the intricacies related to church/state issues. He, probably more than anyone else in China, opened my eyes to what truly is going on in China.

One of his greatest achievements was to help write the passage on religious freedom in China's new constitution.[98] He also was responsible for establishing the Amity Printing Company so that Bibles could be printed again legally in China. As of January 2005, 40,417,527 Bibles and New Testaments have rolled off the press at the Amity Printing Company in Nanjing alone. (Since the Cultural Revolution over 42 million Bibles and New Testaments have been printed, if you count those that have been printed in other printing companies.)

On the other hand, one of China's pastors confided in me, "I don't understand my bishop anymore." Ting's liberal theology has gone too far for him and many others.

The bishop does not like to differentiate between evangelical and liberal Christians. In one of his letters to me he wrote, "You surprised me greatly when I saw a copy of your September circular letter to your 'ministry friends' which arbitrarily divides Chinese Protestant Christians as 'evangelicals' (90 percent) and 'liberals.' The latter you define and vilify as those in our church who can only listen to government orders. So you turn a religious difference into a political one."

And this is the only area where I have my concern: liberalism. Liberal theology, whether in China or any other part of the world, will eventually lead the church to falter and fail. When dialoguing with Bishop Ting on these issues, I vividly remember saying, "As a German I am deeply disturbed when liberal theology enters the church. Much of liberal theology had its beginning in Germany, and

---

[98] See appendix 6, chapter 2, article 36.

liberal theology emptied our churches. You don't want to have this happen in China."

The bishop disagrees with me on several matters. On many other issues, however, we do agree. He wrote me on September 25, 1999, "So, at this stage, the least we have to require of you is: in Hunan, Jiangxi, and anywhere else you go to in China, you declare to your listeners clearly that you honor the Christian unity advocated by the CCC, and that Christians need not all hold to exactly the same theological points of view as long as we hold to the Lordship of Jesus Christ as taught by the Bible."

The debate on theological (re)construction will go on. I pray that it will stir Christians in China to reexamine how they can best reach their fellow citizens and not let them succumb to unbiblical teaching.

Toward Better Theology

Christians in the West can be helpful by keeping a positive attitude about this inner struggle. As followers of Jesus, representing Him in different world areas, we sympathize with our Chinese fellow believers. Not one Christian group anywhere in the world has not had similar struggles. Sometimes it tore believers and entire denominations apart; other times such struggles produced better theology. All of us should strive for the latter.

But how? At a time when the explosive growth of the Chinese church produces all types of theological thinking—some of it good and biblical, others liberal and questionable, and still others weird and detrimental—Christians must be alert. Here is where the rest of the world can lend a hand, but this needs to be done in a "give and take" manner.

Let me point out two areas where we can learn from each other. The first one shows how the Chinese Christians can help and even teach us in the area of suffering, and the second one highlights the subject of bureaucracy, where we from the West can assist our friends in China.

Chinese Christians can teach us much about the theology of suffering. I shall never forget my first and only ministry trip to Jinan in the province of Shandong. Our China Partner teaching team had been invited to lecture at the newly reopened theological seminary that had been closed during the gruesome period of the Cultural Revolution. The president of the seminary, then in his eighties, exuded a heartwarming spirit of love. After hearing our gospel singer Ed Lyman, also known as the singing marine, the now deceased Bishop Wang was so touched by the old gospel hymns that he wanted more of them.

He himself was quite a musician. "I remember singing many of those hymns in my early years of ministry," he said, "but we lost all of the old hymnals during the Cultural Revolution. I would love to have a hymnal published by Sankey, the famous gospel singer of Dwight L. Moody. My, could he sing. And then the wonderful songs he wrote! Those songs and hymns kept us sane in those dark days of trial. Do you know whether it is still in print? If so, can you get it for me?"

I did not know but promised to find out.[99] Then he shared with us some of the horrors he and all Christians had endured. The persecution at that time was almost unbearable. "Many of us suffered deeply," he said, "but we learned how to bear suffering. It was so intense that I understood for the first time what it truly means to go through the valley of the shadow of death.[100] It was our 'sacrament of suffering.'"

[99] Upon my return home, while talking on the phone with Mrs. Ruth Graham, I shared the bishop's wish with her. "Wait a minute," she said, "I may have that hymnal." A couple of hours later she called back and said, "I found two of them. Many years ago Bill (that's how she refers to her husband) and I picked them up in London in a store for antique books. Let me send you one." She and Billy signed their names on the cover page, and I had the joy of passing it on to Bishop Wang.

[100] Psalm 23.

Suffering is connected to the biblical teaching of the cross. Martin Luther, one of the world's greatest reformers, was also known as the theologian of the cross. The cross was the centerpiece of Christ's suffering. Luther understood deeply what Christ had to go through when he was harassed, beaten, spat upon, ridiculed, and finally nailed to the cross.[101] That was true suffering. Jesus challenges us to "take up [your] cross daily and follow me."[102] For the Chinese believers suffering became part of their lives. This made them strong and finally enabled them to attract millions of their fellow citizens to the Christian faith.

During that time of suffering, all of their churches and chapels were closed. Christian organizations were banned. Theological schools were closed. Christians had to meet secretly in their own homes. Bibles and hymnals were confiscated and destroyed. Rice Christians[103] disappeared from the scene. Only those who had received new life through Christ and had been born again could withstand the evil forces and persecution.

Thus, the outer trappings of an organized church were stripped away. Bloated bureaucracies so dear to western denominations disappeared. David Mills eloquently describes wrongly cultivated religious bureaucracies to be detrimental to the western church in his article "Reorganizing Religion":

> I am not criticizing bureaucracy as such, because it is natural and inevitable. A bishop begins a diocesan bureaucracy as soon as he hires a secretary or convenes a small group to help him with the finances. But some subtle line is crossed, and crossed quickly, when these people and their work become authorities in their own right and work more by rule and process than personal relation.

---

[101] Mark 10:34.

[102] Luke 9:23, KJV.

[103] Rice Christians were those who became Christians in order to receive favors and benefits doled out by Christian missionaries.

> It is crossed, for example, when the bishop appoints someone because he has to satisfy some political need—to satisfy powerful people in the diocese, for example—not because the man is godly, wise, and discerning. It is generally being crossed when a bishop thinks he is being shrewd.
>
> Bureaucracy is simply one way of getting things done, and the questions to be asked of it are whether it does them well and whether it does other things than it is supposed to do. I want only to suggest that it is not the best form of organization for modern church life.

He concludes his article with a challenge to reform:

> The test of the reform is evangelism: whether the bureaucratic or the personal styles of ministry will reach the world most effectively. The extraordinary growth of the churches in Africa and Asia, where bureaucracies are small and bishops and their priests are usually evangelists as well as pastors, suggests the superiority of the personal to the bureaucratic.
>
> When their churches are growing so rapidly, even as they are persecuted for their faith, the West might wisely defer to their wisdom. It can't claim to have had great success doing things its way. The Western churches might see the beginning of a revival if their bishops filed all the reports and resolutions, dissolved all but the essential committees and canceled the legislative meetings, and went out into the streets of their sees with a bishop from Africa to tell people about Jesus.[104]

We from the West can encourage our Chinese brothers and sisters to study what happened to many of our mainline denominations once they veered from biblical truth and depended upon bureaucracies. Only those local churches that would not follow the trend of their denominational liberal leadership kept themselves alive and on

---

[104] David Mills, "Reorganizing Religion," *Touchtone Magazine* (September 2004): 39.

the cutting edge. Seminaries that continued to teach sound biblical truths are growing. They raise competent pastors who serve thriving evangelical churches. We can humbly point them to books like *The Empty Church: The Suicide of Liberal Christianity*[105] and *Catholicism and Modernity.*[106]

We need to encourage seminary and Bible school students, as well as the pastors across the land and preachers on the lowest level, to shun bureaucratic restrictions from the church hierarchy. Administration is necessary, but it must be kept in check. Administration is necessary, but it should be people and message oriented.

Chinese pastors need to hear from us westerners that religious bureaucracy is not the answer for church growth—neither numerically nor spiritually. Living with Jesus and doing evangelism combined with discipleship training will build the church. "Keep on doing what you are doing," should be our advice.

We can encourage them in other areas. Together with our Chinese friends we can focus on those who will truly make a difference in the battle for minds and hearts.

---

[105] Thomas Reeves, *The Empty Church: The Suicide of Liberal* Christianity (New York: The Free Press, 1997).

[106] James Hitchcock, *Catholicism and Modernity* (New York: The Seabury Press, 1979), 96–125.

Chapter 13

A Recap of Christian Ministry in China

Christian ministry activities go back hundreds of years. The Nestorians carried out the first known and recorded missionary involvement in China. Initially they found a receptive audience. Latourette wrote:

> It was through Nestorians that Christianity was introduced to China. The year of the first known coming of Christianity to that vast land was 635. At that time the T'ang Dynasty had recently risen to power and T'ai Tsung, the able monarch of that line, was on the throne. . . . The first missionary, A-lo-pen, came to the capital, Ch'ang-an, the present Hsianfu. In succeeding years Christian monasteries were founded in several cities, Christian literature in Chinese was produced, and a metropolitanate was created for China. Some converts were won, but the core of the Christian communities and perhaps their membership was predominantly foreign.[107]

The church prospered for two hundred years. Under Emperor Wu Tsung in 845, however, persecution began. In a short time the church suffered a crushing blow but was not totally eradicated.

---

[107] Kenneth Scott Latourette, *A History of Christianity* (New York: Harper & Brothers, 1953), 324–25.

Four hundred and fifty years passed before missionaries made another attempt to plant the church in China. It enjoyed some success, but again the Chinese drove out Christians, forced them underground, or killed them as martyrs. Latourette wrote:

> In 1368, the Mongol Dynasty in China came to an end and was succeeded by the Ming Dynasty, founded by a Chinese and brought to power in part by anti-foreign sentiment. This meant the expulsion, the assimilation, or the dying out of the minor foreign communities in China, among them those which professed the Christian faith. Indeed, so completely did Christianity disappear in China that we do not know either the date or the manner of its demise.[108]

Two hundred years later, Matteo Ricci (1552–1610) went to China and became the best known Jesuit missionary and foreign scholar in that land. He won the ear and pleasure of the emperor in Beijing. He developed a strategy to plant the church in China by mixing Christian beliefs with local religions. Garraty wrote:

> In contrast to the Franciscans of the Mongolian era, the highly educated Jesuits who came this time met the Chinese intelligentsia as equals. They were experts in mathematics, astronomy, physics, and geography. One of them, the great Matteo Ricci (1552–1610), was summoned to Peking in 1601 and stayed there until his death. . . . Furthermore, the Jesuits were not only willing to accept positions in the Chinese bureaucracy and to adjust themselves to the Chinese worldview, but also to explain Christianity in Chinese terms. They emphasized the similarities between Christianity and Confucianism, equating the Christian God with the Chinese heaven, and raising no objection to ancestor worship. This explains why the Jesuits made converts in some circles, but also why they left no lasting mark.[109]

---

[108] Ibid., 601.

[109] John A. Garraty, *The Columbia History of the World* (New York: Harper & Row, 1972), 334.

Protestant missions, however, did not enter China until the eighteenth and nineteenth centuries. They succeeded in spreading the gospel first along the eastern seashore and later in the hinterland of China. Using the influence of foreign colonial powers, they advanced with increasing strength into the remotest corners of the vast country. Progress did not come easy, however. Many hurdles had to be overcome.

Missionaries entering China in the wake of foreign secular enterprises did not sit well with Chinese authorities. In fact, it later became detrimental and even damaging. During several epochs, nationalistic and patriotic feelings of the Chinese resulted in attacks on missionaries. These imperialistic endeavors had damaging repercussions as was described by Harry Hamm:

> What foreign imperial powers perpetrated on Chinese territory at this time, even allowing for a good deal of stupid and arrogant behavior on the part of the Chinese, constitutes one of the blackest chapters in the annals of world history. The carving up of the country into spheres of interest, the establishment of extraterritorial concessions in the most important commercial centers, the annexing of border territories by foreign powers, "gunboat diplomacy" in relations with the Chinese government—all these things were hardly calculated to make the Chinese people trust the foreigners and their modern ideas. It would go beyond the scope of this book to describe these historically fatal events in detail, but their effects are still felt in China even today. For the Chinese, the word "imperialism" has associations far beyond anything the concept evokes in other countries, where it has almost become an empty slogan.[110]

Blood was spilled on several occasions. It was not until Mao's coming to power that all missionary activity ceased, however. "Finally China stood up," he declared on October 1, 1949, thereby

---

[110] Harry Hamm, *China*, (Garden City, New York: Doubleday & Company, Inc. 1966), 225.

renouncing anything foreign within China's borders. China wanted to run its own affairs.

To the Chinese, especially to those who followed the Communist line, Christianity was a foreign religion and had to be purged from Chinese soil. Within a couple of years the government expelled thousands of foreign missionaries. Christian leaders in China did not agree with their new political leaders. They argued that the church transcends not only all strata of society but also all national boundaries. The Christian faith, they argued, was initiated by the only true and living God, who "so loved the world, that he gave his only begotten Son, that whosoever believeth in him should not perish, but have everlasting life" (John 3:16, KJV).

In a series of meetings with Zhou Enlai in May 1950, it was made clear that the Chinese Communist Party (CCP) was not necessarily advocating the extinction of Christian religion. He was concerned, however, about the involvement of foreign missions in the affairs of Chinese churches and the imperialistic overlording by non-Chinese organizations. Philip Wickeri writes:

> Zhou's primary interest was in the social function of Christianity in China, and particularly the relationship between the missionary movement and Western imperialism. While acknowledging the positive contributions that Chinese Christians made to the Chinese revolution, Zhou speaks in no uncertain terms about the conscious and unconscious association between the Christian churches and foreign aggression. His point is that the churches must sever their linkages with imperialism if they are to continue to exist in China.[111]

[111] Philip Wickeri, *Seeking the Common Ground* (Maryknoll, New York: Orbis Books, 1988), 95.

Struggling With Religious Forces In China

China has had a long history of varied religions. Confucius (C'ong-fu-tse, 551–479 BC) is the most renowned and revered teacher and sage in China's history. His teachings became a way of life for China's society. Even though Confucianism should not be understood as a religion, many certainly regarded it as such. Confucian thought impregnated and pervaded the culture in China. It influenced scholars throughout centuries and controlled governmental institutions. Garraty evaluated his teachings:

> Basically, he was concerned with the relation of man to man, and declined to engage in metaphysical speculation. As he saw the past, men had lived together in harmony under the sage rulers of the golden age. They had been truthful and wise, good and righteous, and had fulfilled their ceremonial obligations meticulously and with understanding of the moral content. Man had degenerated since then, but he is fundamentally good and can be salvaged through education.[112]

Even though Confucianism was under siege during the Cultural Revolution, today its teachings have been revived.

> For twenty-five centuries, with occasional breaks, Chinese thinking was governed by Confucius' teachings on society, the state, and morals. For centuries Confucianism gave China the strength to survive in an overpopulated world. It was based on the search for accord and harmony, and it had no room for a turbulent dynamic. Its main components were not basic questions of metaphysics or epistemology, but the shaping of one's daily life by the principles of harmonious order. Pedantic rules of ritual were more important than the nonconformist seeking after the unknowable for its own

[112] Garraty, *Columbia History*, 115–16.

> sake. The family and the clan were regarded as the basic unit of society, the yardstick of one's existence and the sole authority. They were the concern of every individual, and only in them was individual and social security to be found. This attitude of mind was necessarily reflected in the social and state order. Custom and usage counted for more than law. The rulers were the closely-knit upper class, the gentry, trained in ethics, philosophy, and history. The concept of the state and the nation in the real sense was unknown to the Chinese.
>
> Confucius and his teachings are still firmly rooted in the Chinese—and particularly in the way they think of the family and the clan—even if they are only dimly conscious of it and even if it is much diluted.[113]

Buddhism entered China around AD 65. It soon became a driving force in religious life, spreading rapidly across China. Monasteries and temples were built. Probably no other religion has so strongly influenced the Chinese as this one. Buddhism introduced a multitude of gods. People literally fell under the spell of this religion. Garraty noted:

> Buddhism had entered China as a foreign religion, and its enemies continued to look upon it as alien. It was successful because it responded to spiritual needs adapted to Chinese conditions, compromising as Confucianism and Taoism had before it. The more sinified Buddhism became, the less it had in common with the teaching of the Buddha, and eventually it degenerated. But before its spiritual and economic collapse, Buddhism lastingly influenced the thought and art of China.[114]

---

[113] Hamm, *China*, 180–81.

[114] Ibid., 135.

Taoism[115] has many adherents. Temples in honor of emperors and other leading rulers were built across the nation. Often the most scenic spots were chosen, and hundreds of thousands of pilgrims visit those places and kowtow to their gods. Taoists have a philosophy of their own. Herbert Kane wrote:

> Taoism takes its name from the word *tao*, which literally means way, path, or road. It is often translated as truth, doctrine, word, or law. It is the central thought in the *Tao Teh Ching*, the sacred book of Taoism, which is supposed to contain the teachings of the founder, Lao-Tze, who was contemporary with Confucius. There are two forms of Tao, the Tao of Heaven and the Tao of Man. The Tao of Heaven represents the Absolute, the eternal and ubiquitous impersonal Principle by which the universe consists of two souls, or breaths, one called *Yang* and the other, *Yin*. Every physical phenomenon in the universe—the stars in their courses, the earth on its axis, the phases of the moon, the rotation of the seasons—is the result of the interaction of the *Yang* and the *Yin*.[116]

In the western part of China, Islam made significant inroads. In recent years proponents of this religion have become more militant, and the government keeps a watchful eye on them.

With such a formidable array of entrenched religions, the Christian faith took root very slowly. Missionaries often labored for ten, twenty, or even thirty years before converts were made. The devil and his evil forces fought the invasion of the gospel of Christ every

---

[115] "The central objective of Taoism may be said to be a long and serene life. This, as taught by Lao Tzu, is to be obtained through simplicity, tranquility, and enlightenment; as taught by Yang Chu, through escape from injury and the preservation of the essence of one's being; and as taught by Chuang Tzu, through companionship with nature, spiritual freedom, and indifference to life and death. This philosophical Taoism assumed momentum in the third century BC and has continued to the present time." William Theodore de Bary, ed., *Sources of Chinese Tradition* (New York: Columbia University Press, 1960), 256.

[116] Herbert Kane, *A Global View of Christian Missions* (Grand Rapids: Baker Book House, 1985), 210.

inch of the way. By 1850, only 50,000 Chinese Christians lived in all of China. By 1900, its constituency had grown to 80,000. According to some estimates, by 1950 China had only an estimated 700,000 Protestant Christians—a mere 0.2 percent of its population. Many Chinese viewed Christianity as a foreign religion that needed to be resisted.

The church also grew slowly because of other factors. Let's look at three forces that resisted the spread of Christianity in China: foreign business interests, the rise of nationalism, and the rise of communism.

Foreign Business Interests In China

For many centuries European powers had tried to expand their realm of influence into new world areas. Imperialism and colonialism were the order of the day. During the past two to three centuries, China was also subjected to this attempt.

Trade is vital to the development of any nation. Foreign powers saw in China a huge market and therefore forced the Chinese to do business with them. Being a proud and somewhat reserved nation, China resisted the overtures of foreigners. China did not want to be infected with foreign practices.

The most infamous intrusion of a foreign power was Great Britain's demand to import opium into China. Great Britain wanted to extract silver (dollars) from the Chinese in exchange for opium. They imposed the drug upon unscrupulous Chinese businessmen. This degenerative drug turned into one of the most dangerous and malicious threats to China's society. The emperor demanded a stop to this trade, but when the British merchants under the protection of their government refused to give in, the Chinese authorities confiscated and destroyed several tons of drugs.

The British government intervened and sent her armed forces against the Chinese. Ill-equipped Chinese soldiers were no match for the British, and thus China lost the Opium War (1839–1842). Britain forced unequal treaties upon the Chinese. They had to open up certain ports and the Yangtze River to foreign trade. In fact, they had to relinquish their judicial rights to foreigners in several key cities. Opium trade was legalized. The propagation of the Christian faith by missionaries in the interior had to be permitted.

This is one of the dark pages of British colonialism. Other foreign powers soon entered the scene, trying to grab part of the spoils. As a result anti-foreign sentiments ran extremely high.

Rise Of Nationalism

The Chinese had always resented foreign hegemony. National and patriotic feelings erupted, and many called their compatriots to open rebellion. Their pride had been hurt, and they believed that foreign dominion could be thrown off through patriotic nationalism.

From 1850 to 1873, China was thrown into political convulsions. The Taiping Rebellion was one of the most effective but devastating uprisings against the rulers of the Qing (Manchu) Dynasty. Hong Xiuquan (1814–1864), its leader, led the revolution. He had been influenced by Protestant missionaries and through visions was led to believe he was the younger brother of Jesus Christ. He worked to free China from evil forces, such as the Manchus, Taoists, Buddhists, and Confucians.

Many of the political leaders saw in this revolution a threat to Confucian tradition and the existing social structure.[117] Finally, they evicted Hung from his stronghold in Nanjing. After a tremendous amount of bloodshed, the revolution was ultimately brought to an end.

---

[117] Garraty, *Columbia History*, 941.

Rise Of Communism

The Chinese nationalists placed much blame at the feet of the rulers of the Qing Dynasty. In 1911, the Qing Dynasty (also known as Ta Ch'ing Dynasty) was overthrown. On January 1, 1912, Dr. Sun Yat-sen was inaugurated as the first president of the new republic. F. L. Hawks Pott wrote:

> Thus ended the Ta Ch'ing Dynasty. It had "exhausted the Mandate of Heaven." A race that in the beginning had been virile and skilled in the art of war had gradually become effete and utterly corrupt. The mistakes of the Manchus had been many. They had never completely identified themselves with the Chinese and had ruled them as a conquered people. They had become utterly selfish, caring more for the preservation of themselves than for the welfare of the people. Their policy had been shortsighted in the extreme and instead of taking the lead in the development of a Constitutional form of government demanded by the people, they had attempted to stifle the national aspirations. During their rule, China had been subjected to repeated humiliations at the hands of foreign powers, and it is no wonder that they came to be thoroughly hated and mistrusted.[118]

After only one decade, however, some disenchanted and disappointed nationalists believed communism was the only answer to the troubles in China. In July 1923 the first Communist Party Congress convened secretly in Shanghai. This began one of the bloodiest periods in China's history.

The Communist Party, constantly under attack by the forces of the Kuomintang (Chiang Kai-chek's party), grew rapidly. Mao won the hearts of the peasants. He established his first Soviet republic

---

[118] F. L. Hawks Pott, *A Sketch of Chinese History* (Shanghai: Kelly and Walsh, Limited, 1923), 210.

in the province of Jiangxi. Chiang Kai-shek eventually forced him and his forces out. The famous Long March took them through nine provinces. Only about 10,000 out of the initial force of 100,000 marchers reached Yanan in northern China. But Mao displayed an amazing agility and fortitude. He overcame seeming insurmountable odds and prevailed as victor.

Following the Sino-Japanese war from 1937–1945, a most cruel civil war erupted. On October 1, 1949, Mao inaugurated a new Chinese era. "China finally stood up," he declared. China would prove to the world that it could run its own affairs.

Development Of The Protestant Church In China

After early missionary endeavors had come to a standstill, several hundred years passed before Protestants saw the need to evangelize China. In 1807, Robert Morrison from Scotland settled in Canton. Twelve years later he had completed the translation of the entire Bible. Only ten Chinese had joined the church in his first twenty-five years of missionary service, however.

By 1889, the missionary force to China had become international, representing many denominations. Over forty agencies worked in several provinces. One of the largest was the China Inland Mission founded by Hudson Taylor.

G. Thompson Brown writes about the missionaries' desire to alleviate the suffering so prevalent in China:

> From its inception Protestant mission work included a wide variety of responses to human need. The poverty of the peasants, the callous indifference of many officials, and the crushing burden of

> traditional practices were compelling reasons for this. Whenever possible the mission station included a school and a hospital or dispensary.[119]

The missionaries made many friends, and authorities often looked upon their work favorably. The protection missionaries received from their own governments was a bone of contention, however. Brown remarks:

> In spite of all their good works, the missionaries had not been able to rid themselves of the taint of foreignness. Christianity was still a foreign religion, and its foreignness, rather than any distinctive Christian dogma or practice, made it offensive. As the human body reacts to a foreign object in its bloodstream and seeks to reject it, so the Chinese body politic was reacting to the foreign presence in its midst.[120]

One of the fiercest outbreaks against foreigners occurred in the northern province of Shandong. The Boxers, a secret society with religious and political objectives, ruthlessly persecuted foreigners and their Chinese friends. Originally established around 1770, the society first conspired against the reigning royal family and later turned against foreigners. In 1900, when the imperial government openly recognized the society, it spread quickly across the northeast of China. During this period the Boxer Rebellion claimed the lives of over 200 foreign missionaries and their children and over 30,000 Chinese converts or sympathizers. Many died because of their devotion to Christ and in answer to His call.

Despite the persecution, the Chinese church grew at an accelerated rate. Seeming setbacks turned out to be forward thrusts for Christ's kingdom. But more difficult times lay ahead.

---

[119] G. Thompson Brown, *Christianity in the People's Republic of China* (Atlanta: John Knox Press, 1983), 33.
[120] Ibid., 36.

After the catastrophic civil war between the Nationalists and Communists from1925–1949, China had to restructure the entire nation with its federal, provincial, county, and municipal governments. All foreigners with a few exceptions, and with them missionaries, were slowly and ultimately forced out of the country. Thousands of missionaries representing countless mission societies had to leave their labor of love. Missionary endeavors in China seemed to come to an end.

Persecution Of Christian Leaders

Between 1950 and 1976 the churches in China suffered severe pressure and persecution. The Chinese Communist Party considered religion to be an opiate for the people (Karl Marx). Religions, therefore, had to be stamped out. The government scrutinized all pastors and church leaders and imprisoned some of them. Others were executed. Still others were sent into the countryside to work among farmers and in factories, or they were detained in labor camps. Membership in churches dwindled.

During the Cultural Revolution (1966–76), the government eventually closed all churches, Christian schools, theological institutions, and Christian humanitarian agencies, such as orphanages, schools for the blind, and hospitals.

Those early years of communist rule, especially the years of the Cultural Revolution, made it impossible to carry on an effective teaching and training program. Thus a gap of some thirty years (1950–80) developed, even though the foremost theological seminary in Nanjing did not close its doors until 1966. Many pastors in the newly opened churches were over seventy years old. Within the next five to ten years most of them will have retired or gone to heaven. Who will take their place?

After the death of Mao Zedong, much of the blame for the Cultural Revolution was put on four Communist leaders who were prominently active during those years. Mao's wife was one of them. After some vigorous legal maneuvering, they were sentenced to life imprisonment.

With the overthrow of the Gang of Four, new and positive opportunities opened up for China. The new leadership was free to develop an "open door" policy, which, as seen later, was extremely helpful for the church.

New Constitution Of 1982

To bring back some sanity to its political scene, Chinese leaders set forth a new constitution. They initiated new freedoms in it, including religious freedom. The National People's Congress adopted it on December 4, 1982. One of its articles states:

> Citizens of the People's Republic of China enjoy freedom of religious belief. No state organ, public organization, or individual may compel citizens to believe in or not to believe in any religion; nor may they discriminate against citizens who believe in or do not believe in any religion. The state protects legitimate religious activities. No one may make use of religion to engage in activities that disrupt public order, impair the health of citizens, or interfere with the educational system of the state. Religious bodies and religious affairs are not subject to any foreign domination.

Many Christians in China are content but not completely satisfied with the interpretations of this document. What they experience now is relative freedom, but it is better than what they had in the 1950s, 1960s, and 1970s. They try to live out their faith within the confines of given government and state laws.

The communist leadership recognized their country's inadequacy in lifting China out of her misery. China needed the expertise and funding of capitalistic countries. With the embracing of new business policies, the government opened the doors to western culture and religion. With it a new day dawned for the Chinese church. Adeney wrote:

> Christians around the world are thankful for the measure of freedom currently granted by the Chinese government. No longer is Christianity an alien religion. Therefore, instead of the ruthless persecution that characterized the Cultural Revolution, Christians now face the danger inherent in the country's growing materialism and legalized religion.[121]

Since the founding of the People's Republic of China in 1949, the government has experienced numerous changes. We now face its fourth generation. Mao Zedong was the extreme revolutionary; Deng Xiaoping, the pragmatist—he had worked in France as a young man; Jiang Zemin, the engineer—he had climbed the ranks in politics from being the mayor of Shanghai; and now Hu Jintao, the modernist—a slick-looking man in western designer clothes.

Mao wanted to destroy the old culture. The Cultural Revolution was the darkest period of his reign. Most Chinese look back to this period with great horror. Deng began to build bridges to the West. Jiang carried out the dreams of Deng—his motto was stability. Hu will lead China into the twenty-first century.

Mao attempted to destroy religion. Deng reversed that policy. Jiang tried to dovetail socialism with religious thought. Hu is the unknown, however.

The government most likely will not be able to revert back to the hard-line days. People have experienced too much freedom, and it will be difficult for them to accept anything less. In fact, the next five to seven years may become the most productive years with opportunities of ministry never seen before.

---

[121] David Adeney, *China: The Church's Long March* (Ventura, CA: Regal Books, 1985), 138.

A Wonderful Partnership

All of us working in China today face new challenges. These challenges are God-given and worth accepting. As I look back on my China involvement, I praise God for the many wonderful, meaningful working relationships we have enjoyed with our Christian brothers and sisters there. The name of our organization, China Partner, truly reflects this partnership. We have gone to serve the church in China—we have not gone with our own agenda. The Chinese church leadership challenged us to train emerging young Christian leaders, and we accepted it. I shall never forget what Bishop Ting told me years ago. "Let's try it; let's do it."

Two major factions exist in the church in China—the registered church and the unregistered church. Some have the wrong concept that true Christians can be found only in the unregistered church or so-called house churches. That is wrong. After having traveled and ministered all over China since 1981, I learned that millions of Christians in the registered churches are also evangelical, Bible centered, and true followers of Jesus. We have joined hands with these brothers and sisters in Christ.

Westerners working with the registered churches, however, have to be open, transparent, honest, and legal in all of their activities. This is what China Partner has chosen to do. Because of this openness, and in spite of mistakes we have made in the process, we have enjoyed a wonderful togetherness with our Christian friends all across China.

The dangers for the church in China do not come from the Chinese political government as so many in the western world believe; the danger might come from within the church. All the persecution during the Cultural Revolution, and some of it thereafter, did not harm the church in its outreach—it only strengthened it. Liberal teachings from within the church will be disastrous, however. Liberal theology should concern us far more than the Chinese government under which believers live out their faith.

China Partner is committed to stand shoulder to shoulder with our biblically-grounded Chinese brothers and sisters in Christ who work openly and legally. We dare not let them down—we dare not let them down now! We will continue to fellowship with them. We will listen to their concerns. We will answer their calls if help is needed and desired. We will teach or preach when called upon. We ask the Lord to give us wisdom as we pursue the path He has put us on. But we will never interfere with their program, plans, or rightful agenda. By God's grace we will help our brothers and sisters in China to become a glorious church—one without spot, blemish, or wrinkle. On that great day the Chinese church, and those privileged to have had a part in her perfecting, will rejoice.

Epilogue

If Only My Mother Had Been There!

Over 2,000 people jammed the church! If a fire department in the US had arrived at a building filled beyond capacity, and found all the aisles blocked, they would have evacuated the place. But this was a Chinese church. Hundreds more stood outside and listened to the service over loudspeakers. Between 3,000 to 4,000 worshipers had assembled.

We were in Linchuan, a remote town in central Jiangxi, China. Everything seems to be different in China. People there are far more relaxed when it comes to accommodating crowds. Mass meetings are common.

My mother began her missionary career some seventy-five years ago in Linchuan. At that time only a handful of Christians worshiped on Sunday mornings. Few Chinese showed interest in the gospel. They called foreigners—and missionaries—"foreign devils."

A Mighty Work

Today life is different. God is doing a mighty work in China. Over 17,000 churches have reopened or been newly built since the infamous Cultural Revolution—and the Chinese build large churches. Our China Partner team was privileged to witness the grand opening of this newly built house of worship seating 1,800 people. A huge cross on top of the church can be seen from afar. Christians in China want to be seen and heard.

If only my mother could have been there.

Linchuan had seen many upheavals. Chiang Kai-check's troops had fought many battles in this area to oust Mao Zedong from the stronghold he had built in the southern part of this province. That happened in the late 1920s and early 1930s. My parents lived in constant fear and fled from the warring factions many times.

Today Christians assemble freely. They worship in their churches and establish training centers. They preach the gospel without fear, and hundreds come to the Lord. Some churches baptize several hundred new believers each year. We know of churches that have baptized close to 2,000 converts in one year.

If only my mother could have seen the fruit of her labor.

Training centers, Bible schools, and theological seminaries exist. We visited and taught at two of them on our latest trip—one in Nanchang (Jiangxi) and the other in Wuhan (Hubei). These students take copious notes as they listen intently. Looking into the eyes of those eager students brings us great joy.

We also witnessed the dedication of the church in Nanchang. Last year we helped to dedicate the two initial buildings of the Jiangxi Bible School. Within one year they finished a church seating 1,000 people. Initially this was to be a chapel for the students, but then they decided to build a bigger worship center for the community, including Sunday school rooms, a day care center for children and migrant workers, and a medical clinic for students and the general public. Christians from the surrounding areas filled the new building to overflowing. What a thrill to take part in this event. China Partner helped to finance this project.

If only my mother could have seen it.

When my mother met my father in China and decided to serve their Lord together, they never dreamed of what would be accomplished through their combined service. What a privilege for me to see firsthand what has taken place in China. I was born in China, and there I found Christ and dedicated my life to serve Him. My life has come full circle.

"Who Will Go?"

I just laid aside the book *Bob Pierce*[122] written by Franklin Graham with Jeanette Lockerbie. Tears filled my eyes as I read the postscript. Bob had a special place in my heart. As a teenager I committed my life to Christ's service—full time—at one of his meetings in Shanghai. He had challenged us to go all out for Christ—100 percent. This Youth for Christ evangelist had just returned from Korea and poured out his heart as only he could do. His heart's cry came through loud and clear: Let my heart be broken with the things that break the heart of God.

Just days before, he had walked along dusty roads as a fiercely hot sun beat down upon him. He had shared Christ with thousands of Koreans, and many had come to know Christ. Korea had just begun to recover from years of Japanese subjugation. Not many Christians lived there at that time. But the harvest was great.

"Who among you is willing to go?" Bob challenged. "If you will not go, who will go in your place? A lost world is waiting to hear the redeeming message of Christ. The Lord wants you."

I was so moved that I left my seat at the Free Christian Church in Shanghai and walked to the altar. I was willing to go. The time had come for me to dedicate my life to His service. In the ante room I knelt in prayer beside Dick Hillis, a China Inland missionary, who had come to counsel with me. I shall never forget that sacred moment.

As I reread the book about Bob Pierce's life, my heart was strangely warmed once more, but when I came to the postscript I rededicated

---

[122] Franklin Graham with Jeanette Lockerbie, *Bob Pierce, This One Thing I Do* (Waco, Texas: Word Books, 1983).

my life again. Bob was dying of leukemia. During his last days before meeting His Savior, he wrote:

> So many things make me yearn to get on home before the last of the night shades have fallen. It's getting along about sundown, and I must soon hurry to the tool shed and put away my hoe and shovel and all the little implements of the past. There is no sadness in that last walk to the tool shed when you are walking from there into the warmth and light and love of the hearth and home and all the things that the soul most deeply longs for.

Bob Pierce had been a great warrior and worker for the Lord. He had been one of the founders of Youth for Christ and then the founder of World Vision and Samaritan's Purse. As he traveled the back roads of a hurting and dying world, he stretched out his hand of compassion and led people out of their misery into the saving arms of Jesus. Now the time had come for him to go home. He continued:

> I suppose at the end of my life now, I can't really say that I have any regrets. And, one of the sweet things about Jesus is that, the nearer you get to heaven, so many things that you ought to be ashamed of, the Blood has already so cleansed that they don't harass you. There is peace. What if the Lord let the mountain of all your sins become so unbearable that it would kill you? But somehow, in His loving way, He doesn't.

And with moving words he concluded:

> Jesus is so glorious. Heaven is so real; you just can't know how real heaven is. The glory of all of it is that, with all my sins and blunders, I never turned away from the certain knowledge that I was to bring men to Jesus Christ. Everything I ever did that helped a leper or

> an orphan or a widow—the sole, only purpose was not that they might have a better life, but that they might have *eternal life* by the experience of salvation through Jesus Christ, our Lord.[123]

Bob Pierce has gone on to glory. I don't know how long I may still have the privilege to serve my Lord. The shadows in my life grow increasingly longer. But one thing I know. I will follow through with what I had promised on my knees so many years ago in Shanghai, China. It all started in China, and it will end in China, the land of my birth, conversion to Christ, and commitment to His service.

---

[123] Ibid., 216–18.

The Ministry of China Partner

China Partner was founded in 1989 to help meet the spiritual needs in China.

China Partner conducts evangelism, pastoral training, and lay leadership courses in major cities across China.

China Partner sends short-term teaching teams to China conducting Pastoral Training Seminars (PTS) in seminaries, Bible schools, and Bible training centers.

China Partner gives free workbooks and notes to pastors and lay leaders in China.

China Partner provides pastors and theological schools mini-libraries at no charge, including reference Bibles, concordances, Bible handbooks and dictionaries, commentaries, etc.

China Partner uploads to the internet training sessions focusing on the following seminars: evangelism, discipleship, Christian leadership, and pastoral care, covering such lessons as "Communicating the Evangelistic Message—Presentation," "Maintaining Spiritual Freshness Through a Devotional Life of Prayer and Study," "Principles of Discipleship," "Mark of a Disciple," "Practical Wisdom for Pastoral Leadership," and lessons on various pastoral issues.

China Partner ministers to Chinese scholars who are studying in North America with the ultimate goal of reaching them with the gospel of Jesus Christ and discipling them. When they return to China, they are potential Christian leaders and influencers of China's future.

China Partner supports Bible school students and grassroots pastors in poverty-stricken parts of China.

China Partner assists in the construction of new churches and Bible school campuses in China.

China Partner builds bridges of friendship, understanding, and communication with the church in China.

China Partner conducts China Symposiums and China Insight Seminars to educate and inform Christians in the West regarding the current church situation in China. The goal is to encourage Christians to pray more effectively for China and to help them participate with their Chinese brothers and sisters in the efforts to reach China with the gospel.

Our Vision: We envision Chinese with the love for Christ, an understanding of the power of God's Word so they can spread the gospel throughout China and the world.

Our Mission: To serve the church in China as they fulfill the Great Commission.

China Partner, Inc.
mail@chinapartner.org
www.chinapartner.org

* * * * *

China Partner has contacts in these nations:

Canada, canada@chinapartner.org
Germany, germany@chinapartner.org
Hong Kong, hongkong@chinapartner.org
New Zealand, newzealand@chinapartner.org
Switzerland, switzerland@chinapartner.org
United States, info@chinapartner.org

Appendix 1

Provisions on the Administration of Religious Activities of Aliens within the Territory of the People's Republic of China

Decree No. 144 Of The State Council Signed By Premier Li Peng On January 31, 1994

Article 1. These provisions are formulated in accordance with the Constitution in order to ensure the freedom of religious belief of aliens within the territory of the People's Republic of China and to maintain the public interests of the society.

Article 2. The People's Republic of China respects the freedom of religious belief of aliens within Chinese territory and protects friendly contacts and cultural and academic exchanges of aliens with Chinese religious circles in respect of religion.

Article 3. Aliens may participate in religious activities at Buddhist monasteries, Taoist temples, mosques, churches, and other sites for religious activities within Chinese territory. Aliens may preach and expound the scripture at Chinese sites for religious activities at the invitation of Chinese religious bodies at or above the level of provinces, autonomous regions, and municipalities directly under the Central Government

Article 4. Aliens may hold religious activities attended by aliens at the sites for religious activities approved by the department of religious affairs of the people's government at or above the county level.

Article 5. Aliens within Chinese territory may invite Chinese religious personnel to conduct such religious ceremonies as baptism, weddings, funerals, and Taoist and Buddhist rites.

Article 6. Aliens entering Chinese territory may carry religious printed matter, religious audio-visual products, and other religious articles for personal use; if the amount of such religious printed matters, religious audio-visual products, and other religious articles is greater than for personal use, it shall be dealt with in accordance with the provisions of the Chinese Customs.

Religious printed matter or religious audio-visual products whose contents are detrimental to the public interests of Chinese society are forbidden to bring into Chinese territory.

Article 7. Aliens within Chinese territory shall recruit the persons to study abroad to be trained as religious personnel, or come to study or teach at Chinese religious institutions in accordance with the relevant provisions of China.

Article 8. Aliens who conduct religious activities within Chinese territory shall abide by Chinese laws and regulations and shall not establish religious organizations, set up religious offices or sites for religious activities, or run religious institutions within Chinese territory, nor may they develop followers, appoint religious personnel, or engage in other missionary activities.

Article 9. Where aliens conduct religious activities that violate these Provisions, the department of religious affairs and other related departments of the people's government at or above the county level shall dissuade or stop them; where those activities violate the control of the entry and exit of aliens or administration of public security, the public security organs shall punish them in accordance with the law; where a crime is constituted, they shall be investigated for their criminal responsibility by the judicial organs.

Article 10. These Provisions are applicable to religious activities of foreign bodies within Chinese territory.

Article 11. Chinese citizens residing abroad within Chinese territory, Taiwan residents on the Mainland, and the residents of Hong Kong and Macao in the inland, shall conduct religious activities with reference to these Provisions.

Article 12. The department of religious affairs of the State Council shall be responsible for the interpretation of these Provisions.

Article 13. These Provisions shall enter into force as of the day of promulgation.[124]

---

[124] "Regulations on Religious Affairs," ISBN 7-80123-663-7. This booklet is in Chinese and English and was published in China in 2005.

Appendix 2

Rules for the Implementation of the Provisions on the Administration of Religious Activities of Aliens within the Territory of the People's Republic of China

Decree No. 1 by the State Administration for Religious Affairs Signed by General-Director Ye Xiaowen on September 26, 2000

Article 1. These Rules are formulated in accordance with the Provisions on the Administration of Religious Activities of Aliens within the Territory of the People's Republic of China.

Article 2. Aliens within the territory of the People's Republic of China refer to those who are within Chinese territory without Chinese nationalities pursuant to the Nationality Law of the People's Republic of China, including long-term residing China personnel and short-term visiting China personnel.

Article 3. Religious activities of aliens within Chinese territory refer to the religious ceremonies that aliens conduct or participate in according to their own religious belief customs, the contacts with Chinese religious bodies, sites for religious activities, and religious personnel in respect of religion and other relevant activities.

Article 4. The People's Republic of China respects the freedom of religious belief of aliens within Chinese territory, and protects and administrates the religious activities of aliens within Chinese territory in accordance with law.

The People's Republic of China protects friendly contacts and cultural and academic exchanges of aliens within Chinese religious circles in respect of religion in accordance with law.

Article 5. Aliens may participate in religious activities at Buddhist monasteries, Taoist temples, mosques, and churches lawfully registered within Chinese territory according to their own religious belief.

Article 6. At the invitation of Chinese religious bodies at or above the level of province, autonomous region, or municipality directly under the Central Government, aliens visiting China as religious personnel may preach and expound the scripture at lawfully registered sites for religious activities.

At the invitation of Chinese religious bodies at or above the level of province, autonomous region, or municipality directly under the Central Government, and after approval by the departments of religious affairs of the people's governments at or above the provincial level, aliens entering China as other status may preach and expound the scripture at lawfully registered sites for religious activities.

Foreign religious personnel who are invited to preach and expound the scripture at the lawfully registered sites for religious activities shall abide by the administrative rules of these sites and respect the belief customs of the personnel of these sites.

Article 7. The collective religious activities of aliens within Chinese territory shall be conducted at the Buddhist monasteries, Taoist temples, mosques, and churches recognized by the departments of religious affairs of the people's government at or above the county level, or at the temporary sites appointed by the departments of religious affairs of the people's governments of province, autonomous region, or municipality directly under the Central Government.

Where aliens within Chinese territory collectively conduct religious activities at temporary sites, they shall be administrated by the departments of religious affairs of the people's governments at or above the county level.

Article 8. The friendly contacts and cultural and academic exchanges of aliens with Chinese religious circles shall be conducted via Chinese religious bodies at or above the level of province, autonomous region, or municipality directly under the Central Government.

Article 9. Foreign religious organizations that have no corresponding legitimate Chinese religious organizations within Chinese territory and their members must get consent from the departments of religious affairs of the people's governments at provincial level and approval from the State Administration for Religious Affairs before conducting contacts in the name of these organizations or as religious personnel with relevant departments of Chinese government or Chinese religious circles.

Article 10. Consented by Chinese religious bodies, aliens within Chinese territory may invite Chinese religious personnel to conduct such religious ceremonies as baptism, weddings, funerals, and Taoist or Buddhist rites according to each religious customs. Among these ceremonies, the aliens conducting weddings must be males and females who have already set up marriage relationship in accordance with law.

The Chinese religious personnel refer to those who have been recognized and recorded by lawfully registered religious bodies.

Article 11. Consented by national religious bodies or relevant religious bodies at the level of province, autonomous region, or municipality directly under the Central Government, and approved by the departments of religious affairs of the local people's governments at or above the provincial level, aliens entering Chinese territory may carry religious articles used in religious cultural and academic exchanges in accordance with relevant programs and agreements of religious cultural and academic exchanges.

Where the religious articles conform to the stipulations of the previous paragraph and the relevant provisions of the Chinese customs, they shall be passed by the customs based on the certificates issued by the departments of religious affairs of the people's governments of province, autonomous region, and municipality directly under the Central Government of the State Administration for Religious Affairs.

Article 12. It is prohibited to bring the following religious printed matter, religious audio-visual products, and other articles into Chinese territory:

- if the amount exceeds that for personal rational use, and they do not belong to the category stipulated in Article 11;
- if the contents of these articles are detrimental to Chinese national security and public interest of Chinese society.

Where the religious printed matters, religious audio-visual products, and other religious articles are found to be those mentioned in previous paragraph, the case shall be dealt with by the customs in accordance with law.

Where the religious printed matters, religious audio-visual products, and other religious articles that violate the stipulations of the first paragraph have been brought into Chinese territory or transported into Chinese territory by other means, once being found, they shall be dealt with by the departments of religious affairs or other related departments of the people's governments at or above the county level in accordance with law.

Article 13. The enrollment of study abroad or capital provided to China by foreign organizations or individuals for the purpose of training religious personnel shall be accepted by Chinese national religious bodies on the basis of need, and the study abroad personnel shall be selected and dispatched by Chinese national religious bodies as a whole plan.

Foreign organizations or individuals may not recruit students within Chinese territory for their study and training abroad as religious personnel without permission.

Article 14. Aliens who intend to come to China for studying at Chinese religious institutions must conform to the stipulations set by the Provisions on the Administration of Accepting Foreign Students by Chinese Institutions of Higher Learning, get approval from Chinese national religious bodies, and keep records at the State Administration for Religious Affairs.

Article 15. Aliens who intend to come to China for teaching at Chinese religious institutions must be subject to the Methods of Engaging Foreign Professionals by Religious Institutions.

Article 16. Aliens who conduct religious activities within Chinese territory shall abide by Chinese laws and regulations.

Aliens may not intervene in the establishment and change of Chinese religious bodies or sites for religious activities; the selecting, appointing, and changing of religious personnel by Chinese religious bodies; nor may they intervene in or manipulate other internal affairs of Chinese religious bodies.

Within Chinese territory, aliens may not establish religious organizations, institute religious offices, set up sites for religious activities, run religious institutions, or hold religious classes in any names or forms.

Article 17. Aliens may not engage in the following missionary activities within Chinese territory:

- appointing religious personnel among Chinese citizens;
- developing religious followers among Chinese citizens;
- preaching and expounding the scripture at the sites for religious activities without permission;
- preaching and expounding the scripture or conducting religious gathering activities at the places outside the lawfully registered sites for religious activities;
- conducting religious activities in which Chinese citizens are admitted to participate at the temporary sites for religious activities, except that the Chinese religious personnel are invited to preside the religious activities;

- producing or selling religious books and journals, religious audio-visual products, religious electronic goods, or other religious articles;
- distributing religious promotional materials;
- other missionary activities.

Article 18. Where the international religious organizations, offices, and their members intend to contact or conduct other related activities with Chinese religious bodies, sites for religious affairs, and religious personnel, they shall make applications to the departments of religious affairs of the people's governments at or above the provincial level in advance. The contact or other related activities may be conducted only after approval by the departments of religious affairs of the people's governments at or above the provincial level.

Article 19. Where aliens within Chinese territory conduct religious activities that violate these Rules, the departments of religious affairs and other related departments of the people's governments at or above the county level shall stop them in accordance with law.

Where religious activities, conducted by aliens within Chinese territory violate these Rules as well as the Law of the Control on the Entry and Exit of Aliens of the People's Republic of China and the Regulations on Administrative Penalties for Public Security, the aliens shall be dealt with by the public organs in accordance with law; where a crime is constituted, the aliens shall be investigated for their criminal liability by the judicial organs in accordance with law.

Article 20. These Rules are applicable to religious activities conducted by foreign organizations within Chinese territory.

Article 21. The State Administration for Religious Affairs shall be responsible for the interpretation of these Rules.

Article 22. These Rules shall enter into force as of the date of promulgation.[125]

---

[125] Ibid.

APPENDIX 3:

Legislative Resolution on Banning Heretic Cults

DECREE NO. 1 BY THE STATE ADMINISTRATION FOR RELIGIOUS AFFAIRS SIGNED BY GENERAL-DIRECTOR YE XIAOWEN ON SEPTEMBER 26, 2000

Beijing, October 30, 1999—The Twelfth Session of the Standing Committee of the National People's Congress (NPC) today adopted a resolution concerning the banning of heretic cult organizations, prevention measures against them, and punishment for cult activities.

The following is the full text of the NPC resolution:[126]

To maintain social stability, protect the interest of people, safeguard reform and opening up and the construction of a modern socialist country, it is necessary to ban heretic cult organizations and prevent and punish cult activities.

[126] *China Daily,* October 13,1999.

Based on the Constitution and other related laws, the following decision is hereby made:

1. Heretic cult organizations shall be resolutely banned according to law and all of their criminal activities shall be dealt with severely.
   Heretic cults, operating under the guise of religion, Qigong, or other illicit forms, which disturb social order and jeopardize people's life and property, must be banned according to law and punished resolutely.
   People's courts, people's procuratorates, public security, national security, and judicial administrative agencies shall fulfill their duties in carrying out these tasks.
   To be severely dealt with according to law are those who manipulate members of cult organizations to violate national laws and administrative regulations, organize mass gatherings to disrupt social order and fool others, cause deaths, rape women, swindle people out of their money and property, or commit other crimes with superstition or heresy.
2. The principle of combining education with punishment should be followed in order to unify and instruct the majority of the deceived public and to mete out severe punishment to the handful of criminals.
   During the course of handling cult groups according to law, people who joined cult organizations but were unaware of the lies being spread by the group shall be differentiated from criminal elements who organize and take advantage of cult groups for illegal activities and/or to intentionally destroy social stability.
   The majority of the deceived members shall not be prosecuted, while those organizers, leaders, and core members who committed crimes shall be investigated for criminal conduct; those who surrender to the authorities or contribute to the investigations shall be given lesser punishments in accordance with the law or be exempt from punishment.

3. Long-term, comprehensive instruction on the Constitution and the law should be carried out among all citizens, knowledge of science and technology should be popularized, and the national literacy level raised. Banning cult organizations and punishing cult activities according to law goes hand in hand with protecting normal religious activities and people's freedom of religious belief.

   The public should be exposed to the inhumane and anti-social nature of heretic cults so that they can knowingly resist influences of cult organizations, enhance their awareness of the law, and abide by it.
4. All corners of society shall be mobilized in preventing and fighting against cult activities, and a comprehensive management system should be put in place. People's governments and judicial bodies at all levels should be held responsible for guarding against the creation and spread of cult organizations and combating cult activities. This is an important, long-term task that will ensure social stability.

—Translated by Amity News Service (ANS)

Appendix 4

Registration Procedures for Venues for Religious Activities

May 1, 1994

Article 1. These Procedures are formulated in accordance with Article 2 of the "Regulations Governing Venues for Religious Activities."

Article 2. The following conditions must be met to establish a venue for religious activity:

1. There must be a fixed place and name;
2. There must be citizens who are religious believers who regularly take part in religious activities;
3. There must be a management organization composed of citizens who are religious believers;
4. There must be professional clergy or persons who meet the requirements of the particular religious group to conduct religious services;
5. There must be management regulations;
6. There must be a legal source of income.

Article 3. At the time of application for registration, the venue for religious activity must provide the following documentation:

1. An application form;
2. Documentation and credentials related to the venue;
3. The opinion of the village (or township) People's Government or of the city neighborhood committee.

Article 4. The head of the venue's management organization must submit the application for registration, together with the materials required under Article 3, to the Religious Affairs Department of the People's Government at the county level or above.

Article 5. Upon receipt of an application for registration and related materials, the Religious Affairs Department of the People's Government at the county level or above must make a decision on whether to consider the application within fifteen days, on the basis of whether the materials are complete.

Article 6. The Religious Affairs Department of the People's Government at the county level or above will, within sixty days of the decision to consider the application, grant registration and issue a registration certificate to those venues which, based upon investigation and the opinions of related parties, comply with the regulations found in Articles 2 and 3 of these Procedures, and with related provisions in the "Regulations Governing Venues for Religious Activities." Venues which do not fully comply with the regulations will, upon review, be granted temporary registration or deferred registration or be denied registration. They will be notified in writing and given an explanation for the decision.

Article 7. Religious venues registered before the promulgation of these Procedures must exchange their certificate; those which have not been registered should apply for registration according to these Procedures.

Article 8. If a religious venue closes, merges, moves, or otherwise changes the terms which applied at the time of application, its management organization must apply for modification of the certificate to the original issuing body.

Article 9. According to the regulations of the General Civil Law, legally registered venues for religious activities which qualify as juridical persons and which at the same time apply to register as juridical persons, will be issued a certificate of registration as juridical persons. According to the law, a religious venue as a juridical person independently enjoys civil rights and takes on civil responsibilities.

Article 10. A venue's certificate of registration and certificate of registration as a juridical person cannot be changed, transferred, or lent. If the certificate is lost, the venue should report its loss promptly to the original issuing body and apply for a replacement.

Article 11. Upon being granted registration, a venue for religious activity must submit an annual management report to the Religious Affairs Department of the government during the first quarter of each year.

Article 12. The certificate of registration for venues of religious activities and related forms will be uniform and will be issued by the Religious Affairs Bureau of the State Council.

Article 13. Matters not regulated by these Procedures follow the "Regulations Governing Venues for Religious Activities."

Article 14. Interpretation of these Procedures is the provenance of the Religious Affairs Bureau of the State Council.

Article 15. These Procedures take effect from the date of promulgation.

—*Translated by Amity News Service (ANS)*

Appendix 5

Regulations on Religious Affairs

Decree No. 426 Of The State Council Signed By Premier Wen Jiabao On November 30, 2004 (Effective On March 1, 2005)

CHAPTER 1: GENERAL PROVISIONS

Article 1. These Regulations are formulated in accordance with the Constitution and relevant laws for the purposes of ensuring citizens' freedom of religious belief, maintaining harmony among and between religions, preserving social concord, and regulating the administration of religious affairs.

Article 2. Citizens enjoy freedom of religious belief.

No organization or individual may compel citizens to believe in, or not to believe in, any religion; nor may they discriminate against citizens who believe in any religion (hereinafter referred to as religious citizens) or citizens who do not believe in any religion (hereinafter referred to as non-religious citizens).

Religious citizens and non-religious citizens shall respect each other and co-exist in harmony, and so shall citizens who believe in different religions.

Article 3. The State, in accordance with the law, protects normal religious activities and safeguards the lawful rights and interests of religious bodies, sites for religious activities, and religious citizens.

Religious bodies, sites for religious activities, and religious citizens shall abide by the Constitution, laws, regulations, and rules and safeguard unification of the country, unity of all nationalities, and stability of society.

No organization or individual may make use of religion to engage in activities that disrupt public order, impair health of citizens, or interfere with the educational system of the State, or in other activities that harm State or public interests, or citizens' lawful rights and interests.

Article 4. All religions shall adhere to the principle of independence and self-governance. Religious bodies, sites for religious activities, and religious affairs are not subject to any foreign domination.

Religious bodies, sites for religious activities, and religious personnel may develop external exchange on the basis of friendship and equality; all other organizations or individuals shall not accept any religious conditions in external cooperation or exchange in economic, cultural, or other fields.

Article 5. The religious affairs department of the people's government at or above the county level shall, in accordance with the law, exercise administration of religious affairs that involve State or public interests, and the other departments of the people's government at or above the county level shall, in accordance with the law, be responsible for the administration of relevant affairs within the limits of their respective functions and duties.

People's governments at various levels shall solicit the views of religious bodies, sites for religious activities, and religious citizens and coordinate the administration of religious affairs.

CHAPTER 2: RELIGIOUS BODIES

Article 6. The establishment, alteration, or cancellation of registration of a religious body shall be registered in accordance with the provisions of the Regulations on Registration Administration of Associations.

The articles of association of a religious body shall comply with the relevant provisions of the Regulations on Registration Administration of Associations.

The activities carried out by a religious body in accordance with its articles of association are protected by law.

Article 7. A religious body may, in accordance with the relevant provisions of the State, compile and publish reference publications to be circulated within religious circles. Religious publications for public distribution shall be published in accordance with the relevant provisions of the State on publication administration.

Publications involving religious contents shall comply with the provisions of the Regulations on Publication Administration and shall not contain the contents:

- which jeopardize the harmonious co-existence between religious and non-religious citizens;
- which jeopardize the harmony between different religions or within a religion;
- which discriminate against or insult religious or non-religious citizens;
- which propagate religious extremism; or
- which contravene the principle of independence and self-governance in respect of religions.

Article 8. For the establishment of an institute for religious education, an application shall be made by the national religious body to the religious affairs department of the State Council, or made by the religious body of the province, autonomous region, or municipality directly under the Central Government to the religious affairs department of the people's government of the province, autonomous region, or municipality directly under the Central Government of the place where such institute is to be located. The religious affairs department of the people's government of the province, autonomous region, or municipality directly under the Central Government shall, within thirty days from the receipt of the application, put forward its views, and, if it agrees to the establishment, make a report to the religious affairs department of the State Council for examination and approval.

The religious affairs department of the State Council shall, within sixty days from the date of receipt of the application made by the national religious body or the report made by the religious affairs department of the people's government of the province, autonomous region, or municipality directly under the Central Government on the establishment of the institute for religious education, make a decision of approval or disapproval.

Article 9. An institute for religious education to be established shall meet the following conditions:

- having clear and definite training objectives, a charter for school-running, and a curriculum;
- having the source of students who meet the training requirements;
- having the necessary funds for school-running and stable financial sources;
- having the sites, facilities, and equipment for teaching that are necessary for its tasks of teaching and school-running scale;
- having full-time leading members, qualified full-time teachers, and an internal management organization; and
- being rationally distributed.

Article 10. In light of the need of the religion concerned, a national religious body may, in accordance with the relevant provisions, select and send people for religious studies abroad or accept foreigners for religious studies in China.

Article 11. The making of hajj abroad by Chinese citizens who believe in Islam shall be organized by the national religious body of Islam.

CHAPTER 3: SITES FOR RELIGIOUS ACTIVITIES

Article 12. Collective religious activities of religious citizens shall, in general, be held at registered sites for religious activities (i.e., Buddhist monasteries, Taoist temples, mosques, churches, and other fixed premises for religious activities), organized by the sites for religious activities or religious bodies, and presided over by religious personnel or other persons who are qualified under the prescriptions of the religion concerned, and the process of such activities shall be in compliance with religious doctrines and canons.

Article 13. For the preparation for establishing a site for religious activities, an application shall be made by a religious body to the religious affairs department of the people's government at the county level of the place where such site is to be located. The religious affairs department of the people's government at the county level shall, within thirty days from the receipt of the application, make a report to the religious affairs department of the people's government at the level of a city divided into districts for examination and approval if it agrees to the establishment.

Within thirty days from the date of receipt of the report made by the religious affairs department of the people's government at the county level, the religious affairs department of the people's government at the level of a city divided into districts shall, if it agrees to the establishment of a Buddhist monastery, Taoist temple, mosque, or church, put forward its views upon examination and verification and make a report to the religious affairs department of the people's government of the province, autonomous region, or municipality directly under the Central Government for examination and approval; and for the establishment of other fixed premises for religious activities, it shall make a decision of approval or disapproval.

The religious affairs department of the people's government of the province, autonomous region, or municipality directly under the Central Government shall, within thirty days from the date of receipt of the report made by the religious affairs department of the people's government at the level of a city divided into districts agreeing to the establishment of a Buddhist monastery, Taoist temple, mosque, or church, make a decision of approval or disapproval.

A religious body may begin the preparatory work for establishing a site for religious activities only after the application for such establishment is approved.

Article 14. A site for religious activities to be established shall meet the following conditions:

1. it is established for a purpose not in contravention of the provisions of Articles 3 and 4 of these Regulations;
2. local religious citizens have a need to frequently carry out collective religious activities;
3. there are religious personnel or other persons who are qualified under the prescriptions of the religion concerned to preside over the religious activities;
4. there are the necessary funds; and
5. it is rationally located without interfering with the normal production and livelihood of the neighboring units and residents.

Article 15. Upon approval of preparation for the establishment of a site for religious activities and completion of construction, an application shall be made for registration with the religious affairs department of the people's government at the county level of the place where such site is located. The religious affairs department of the people's government at the county level shall, within thirty days from the date of receipt of application, examine the management organization, formulation of internal rules, and other aspects of such site, and, if the site meets the conditions for registration, register it and issue the Registration Certificate of the Site for Religious Activities.

Article 16. When a site for religious activities merges with another one, divides itself, terminates, or changes any item registered, the formalities for alteration registration shall be gone through with the original registration administration department.

Article 17. A site for religious activities shall set up a management organization and exercise democratic management. Members of the management organization of the site for religious activities shall be recommended or elected upon democratic consultation, and then be reported to the registration administration department of such site for the record.

Article 18. A site for religious activities shall strengthen internal management, and, in accordance with the provisions of the relevant laws, regulations, and rules, establish and improve the management systems for personnel, finance, accounting, security, fire control, cultural relics protection, sanitation, and epidemic prevention, etc., and accept the guidance, supervision, and inspection by the relevant departments of the local people's government.

Article 19. The religious affairs department shall supervise and inspect the sites for religious activities in terms of their compliance with laws, regulations, and rules, the development and implementation of management systems, the alterations of registered items, and the conduction of religious activities and activities that involve foreign affairs. The sites for religious activities shall accept the supervision and inspection by the religious affairs department.

Article 20. A site for religious activities may accept donations from citizens in accordance with religious customs, but no means of compulsion or apportionment may be adopted.

No non-religious bodies or sites not for religious activities may organize or hold any religious activities, nor accept any religious donations.

Article 21. Religious articles, artworks, and publications may be sold in the sites for religious activities.

A Buddhist monastery, Taoist temple, mosque, or church that is registered as a site for religious activities (hereinafter referred to as a monastery, temple, mosque, or church) may, in accordance with the relevant provisions of the State, compile and publish reference publications to be circulated within religious circles.

Article 22. Where a large-scale religious activity, in which different provinces, autonomous regions, and municipalities directly under the Central Government are involved and which is beyond the accommodation capacity of a site for religious activities, is to be held, or where a large-scale religious activity is to be held outside a site for religious activities, the religious body, monastery, temple, mosque, or church that sponsors such activity shall, thirty days before the activity is held, make an application to the religious affairs department of the people's government of the province, autonomous region, or municipality directly under the Central Government of the place where such large-scale religious activity is to be held. The religious affairs department of the people's government of the province, autonomous region, or municipality directly under the Central Government shall, within fifteen days from the date of receipt of the application, make a decision of approval or disapproval.

A large-scale religious activity shall, as required in the written notification of approval, proceed in accordance with religious rites and rituals, without violating the relevant provisions of Articles 3 and 4 of these Regulations. The religious body, monastery, temple, mosque, or church that sponsors such large-scale religious activity shall adopt effective measures to prevent against any accidents. The people's government of the township or town and the relevant departments of the local people's government at or above the county level of the place where such large-scale religious activity is to be held shall, within the limits of their respective functions and duties, exercise the necessary administration in order to ensure the safe and orderly progress of the large-scale religious activity.

Article 23. A site for religious activities shall prevent against the occurrence, within the site, of any major accident or event, such as breaking of religious taboos, which hurts religious feeling of religious citizens, disrupts the unity of all nationalities, or impairs social stability.

When an accident or event mentioned in the preceding paragraph occurs, the site for religious activities in question shall, without delay, make a report to the religious affairs department of the people's government at the county level of the place where it is located.

Article 24. Where a religious body, monastery, temple, mosque, or church intends to build a large-size outdoor religious statue outside the site for religious activities, the relevant religious body of the province, autonomous region, or municipality directly under the Central Government shall make an application to the religious affairs department of the people's government of the province, autonomous region, or municipality directly under the Central Government, which shall, within thirty days from the date of receipt of the application, put forward its views, and, if it agrees to the building of such statue, make a report to the religious affairs department of the State Council for examination and approval.

The religious affairs department of the State Council shall, within sixty days from the date of receipt of the report on building a large-size outdoor religious statue outside the site for religious activities, make a decision of approval or disapproval.

No organizations or individuals other than religious bodies, monasteries, temples, mosques, and churches may build large-size outdoor religious statues.

Article 25. Where a unit or an individual intends to alter or construct buildings, set up commercial service centers, hold displays or exhibitions, or make films or television programs in a site for religious activities, it shall obtain in advance the consent of the site for religious activities in question and that of the religious affairs department of the local people's government at or above the county level of the place where such site is located.

Article 26. For a scenic spot or historic zone where a site for religious activities therein constitutes the main tourist attraction, the local people's government at or above the county level of the place where such a spot or zone is located shall coordinate and deal with the interrelated interests between the site for religious activities and the park, relics, and tourism, and safeguard the lawful rights and interests of the site for religious activities.

The planning and construction of a scenic spot or historic zone where a site for religious activities constitutes the main tourist attraction shall be in harmony with the style and surroundings of such site.

CHAPTER 4: RELIGIOUS PERSONNEL

Article 27. Religious personnel who are determined qualified as such by a religious body and reported for the record to the religious affairs department of the people's government at or above the county level may engage in professional religious activities.

The succession of living Buddhas in Tibetan Buddhism shall be conducted under the guidance of Buddhism bodies and in accordance with the religious rites and rituals and historical conventions, and be reported for approval to the religious affairs department of the people's government at or above the level of a city divided into districts, or to the people's government at or above the level of a city divided into districts. With respect to Catholic bishops, the matter shall be reported for the record by the national religious body of the Catholic Church to the religious affairs department of the State Council.

Article 28. Where religious personnel are to assume or leave the chief religious posts of a site for religious activities, the matter shall, upon consent by the religious body of the religion concerned, be reported to the religious affairs department of the people's government at or above the county level for the record.

Article 29. The presiding over religious activities, conduction of religious ceremonies, sorting out of religious scriptures and pursuit of religious and cultural research by religious personnel are protected by law.

CHAPTER 5: RELIGIOUS PROPERTY

Article 30. The land legally used by a religious body or a site for religious activities, the houses, structures, and facilities legally owned or used by such body or site, and its other legal property and proceeds thereof, are protected by law.

No organization or individual may encroach upon, loot, privately divide up, damage, destroy, or illegally seal up, impound, freeze, confiscate, or dispose of the legal property of a religious body or a site for religious activities, nor damage or destroy cultural relics possessed or used by a religious body or a site for religious activities.

Article 31. The houses owned and the land used by a religious body or a site for religious activities shall, according to law, be registered with the real estate department and the land administration department of the local people's government at or above the county level, and be granted the certificate of ownership and the certificate of right to use; where the property right is altered, the formalities for alteration registration shall be gone through without delay.

The land administration department shall, when determining and altering the land-use right of a religious body or a site for religious activities, solicit the views of the religious affairs department of the people's government at the same level.

Article 32. The houses and structures used for religious activities by a site for religious activities, and their accessory houses for the daily use of religious personnel as well, shall not be transferred, mortgaged, or used as investments in kind.

Article 33. Where the houses or structures of a religious body or a site for religious activities need to be demolished or relocated because of city planning or construction of key projects, the demolisher shall consult with the religious body or the site for religious activities concerned, and solicit the views of the relevant religious affairs department. If, after consultation, all the parties concerned agree to the demolition, the demolisher shall rebuild the houses or structures demolished, or, in accordance with the relevant provisions of the State, make compensation on the basis of the appraised market price of the houses or structures demolished.

Article 34. A religious body or a site for religious activities may operate public undertakings according to law, and the proceeds and other lawful income therefrom shall be subject to financial and accounting management, and be used for the activities that are commensurate with the purpose of the religious body or the site for religious activities, or for public undertakings.

Article 35. A religious body or a site for religious activities may, in accordance with the relevant provisions of the State, accept donations from organizations and individuals at home or abroad, which shall be used for the activities that are commensurate with the purpose of the religious body or the site for religious activities.

Article 36. A religious body or a site for religious activities shall implement the systems of the State for administration of financial and accounting affairs and taxation, and may enjoy the preferential treatment in terms of tax reduction or exemption in accordance with the relevant provisions of the State on taxation.

A religious body or a site for religious activities shall report to the religious affairs department of the people's government at or above the county level of the place where it is located on its income and expenditure, and on the acceptance and use of donations as well, and, in an appropriate way, make such information public to religious citizens.

Article 37. In case of cancellation of registration or termination of a religious body or a site for religious activities, the property thereof shall be liquidated and the property remaining after the liquidation shall be used for the undertakings that are commensurate with the purpose of the religious body or the site for religious activities.

CHAPTER 6: LEGAL LIABILITY

Article 38. Where any State functionary, in administration of religious affairs, abuses his power, neglects his duty, or commits illegalities for personal gain or by fraudulent means, and a crime is thus constituted, he shall be investigated for criminal liability according to law; if no crime is constituted, he shall be given an administrative sanction according to law.

Article 39. Where anyone compels citizens to believe in, or not to believe in, any religion, or interferes with the normal religious activities conducted by a religious body or a site for religious activities, the religious affairs department shall order it to make corrections; if such act constitutes a violation of public security administration, it shall be given an administrative penalty for public security according to law.

Where anyone infringes upon the lawful rights and interests of a religious body, a site for religious activities or a religious citizen, it shall assume civil liability according to law; if a crime is constituted, it shall be investigated for criminal liability according to law.

Article 40. Where anyone makes use of religion to engage in such illegal activities as endanger State or public security, infringe upon citizens' right of the person and democratic rights, obstruct the administration of public order, or encroach upon public or private property, and a crime is thus constituted, it shall be investigated for criminal liability according to law; if no crime is constituted, the relevant competent department shall give it an administrative penalty according to law; if any loss is caused to a citizen, legal person, or any other organization, it shall assume civil liability according to law.

Where, in the course of a large-scale religious activity, there occurs any event endangering public security or seriously disrupting public order, the matter shall be handled on the spot and penalties shall be imposed in accordance with the laws and administrative regulations on assembly, procession, and demonstration; if the religious body, monastery, temple, mosque, or church that sponsors such large-scale religious activity is responsible therefore, the registration administration department shall cancel its registration.

Where anyone organizes a large-scale religious activity without approval, the religious affairs department shall order it to discontinue such activities and shall confiscate the illegal gains, if any; and it may concurrently impose thereupon a fine of not less than one time but not more than three times the illegal gains. In addition, if the large-scale religious activity is organized by a religious body or a site for religious activities without approval, the registration administration department may order the religious body or the site for religious activities to dismiss and replace the person-in-charge who is directly responsible therefore.

Article 41. Where a religious body or a site for religious activities commits any of the following acts, the religious affairs department shall order it to make corrections; if the circumstances are relatively serious, the registration administration department shall order the religious body or the site for religious activities to dismiss and replace the person-in-charge who is directly responsible therefore; if the circumstances are serious, the registration administration department shall cancel the registration of such religious body or site for religious activities and confiscate the unlawful property or things of value, if any:

- failing to go through the formalities for alteration registration or submission for the record in accordance with the relevant provisions;
- in the case of a site for religious activities, in violation of Article 18 of these Regulations, failing to formulate relevant management systems, or failing to have the management systems meet the requirements;
- failing to report, without delay, on the occurrence of any major accident or event in a site for religious activities, thus causing serious consequences;

- contravening the principle of independence and self-governance in violation of the provisions of Article 4 of these Regulations;
- accepting donations from home or abroad in violation of the provisions of the State; or
- refusing to accept supervision and administration conducted by the registration administration department according to law.

Article 42. Where any publications involving religious contents contain the contents prohibited by the second paragraph of Article 7 of these Regulations, the relevant competent department shall impose administrative penalties upon the relevant responsible units and persons according to law. If a crime is constituted, criminal liability shall be investigated according to law.

Article 43. Where a site for religious activities is established without approval, or a site originally for religious activities continues to carry out religious activities after its registration as such has been canceled, or an institute for religious education is established without approval, the religious affairs department shall ban such site or institute and confiscate the illegal gain; the illegal houses or structures, if any, shall be disposed of by the competent construction department according to law. If any act in violation of public security administration is committed, an administrative penalty for public security shall be imposed according to law.

Where a non-religious body or a site not for religious activities organizes or holds religious activities or accepts religious donations, the religious affairs department shall order it to discontinue such activities and confiscate the illegal gains, if any; if the circumstances are serious, a fine of not less than one time but not more than three times the illegal gains may be imposed concurrently.

Where anyone organizes the making of hajj abroad for religious citizens without authorization, the religious affairs department shall order it to discontinue such activities and shall confiscate the illegal gains, if any; and it may concurrently impose a fine of not less than one time but not more than three times the illegal gains.

Article 44. Where, in violation of the provisions of these Regulations, anyone builds a large-size outdoor religious statue, the religious affairs department shall order it to discontinue the construction and to demolish the statue in a specified time limit; the illegal gains, if any, shall be confiscated.

Article 45. Where any religious personnel violate laws, regulations, or rules in professional religious activities, the religious affairs department shall, in addition to having the legal liability investigated according to law, make a proposal to the religious body concerned to disqualify them as religious personnel.

Where anyone engages in professional religious activities by impersonating religious personnel, the religious affairs department shall order it to discontinue such activities and shall confiscate the illegal gains, if any; if any act in violation of public security administration is committed, an administrative penalty for public security shall be imposed thereupon according to law; if a crime is constituted, criminal liability shall be investigated according to law.

Article 46. Where anyone refuses to accept a specific administrative act taken by the religious affairs department, it may apply for administrative reconsideration according to law; if it refuses to accept the decision of the administrative reconsideration, it may institute an administrative lawsuit according to law.

CHAPTER 7: SUPPLEMENTARY PROVISIONS

Article 47. The religious exchange between the Mainland and the Hong Kong Special Administrative Region, the Macao Special Administrative Region, and Taiwan region shall be developed in accordance with laws, administrative regulations, and the relevant provisions of the State.

Article 48. These Regulations shall become effective as of March 1, 2005. The Regulations on Administration of Sites for Religious Activities promulgated by the State Council on January 31, 1994 shall be repealed simultaneously.[127]

[127] "Regulations on Religious Affairs."

Appendix 6

Constitution of the People's Republic of China

Adopted On December 4, 1982

PREAMBLE

China is one of the countries with the longest histories in the world. The people of all nationalities in China have jointly created a splendid culture and have a glorious revolutionary tradition. Feudal China was gradually reduced after 1840 to a semicolonial and semifeudal country. The Chinese people waged wave upon wave of heroic struggles for national independence and liberation and for democracy and freedom. Great and earthshaking historical changes have taken place in China in the twentieth century. The Revolution of 1911, led by Dr. Sun Yat-sen, abolished the feudal monarchy and gave birth to the Republic of China. But the Chinese people had yet to fulfill their historical task of overthrowing imperialism and feudalism. After waging hard, protracted, and tortuous struggles, armed and otherwise, the Chinese people of all nationalities, led by the Communist Party of China with Chairman Mao Zedong as its leader, ultimately, in 1949, overthrew the rule of imperialism, feudalism, and bureaucratic capitalism, won the great victory of the new-democratic revolution, and founded the People's Republic of

China. Thereupon the Chinese people took state power into their own hands and became masters of the country.

After the founding of the People's Republic, the transition of Chinese society from a new-democratic to a socialist society was effected step by step. The socialist transformation of the private ownership of the means of production was completed, the system of exploitation of man by man eliminated, and the socialist system established. The people's democratic dictatorship, led by the working class and based on the alliance of workers and peasants, which is in essence the dictatorship of the proletariat, has been consolidated and developed. The Chinese people and the Chinese People's Liberation Army have thwarted aggression, sabotage, and armed provocations by imperialists and hegemonists, safeguarded China's national independence and security, and strengthened its national defense. Major successes have been achieved in economic development. An independent and fairly comprehensive socialist system of industry has in the main been established. There has been a marked increase in agricultural production. Significant progress has been made in educational, scientific, cultural, and other undertakings, and socialist ideological education has yielded noteworthy results. The living standards of the people have improved considerably. Both the victory of China's new-democratic revolution and the successes of its socialist cause have been achieved by the Chinese people of all nationalities under the leadership of the Communist Party of China and the guidance of Marxism-Leninism and Mao Zedong Thought, and by upholding truth, correcting errors, and overcoming numerous difficulties and hardships.

The basic task of the nation in the years to come is to concentrate its effort on socialist modernization. Under the leadership of the Communist Party of China and the guidance of Marxism-Leninism and Mao Zedong Thought, the Chinese people of all nationalities will continue to adhere to the people's democratic dictatorship and follow the socialist road, steadily improve socialist institutions, develop socialist democracy, improve the socialist legal system, and work hard and self-reliantly to modernize industry, agriculture, national defense, and science and technology step by step to turn China into a socialist country with a high level of culture and democracy. The exploiting classes as such have been eliminated in our country. However, class struggle will continue to exist within certain limits for a long time to come. The Chinese people must fight against those forces and elements, both at home and abroad, which are hostile to China's socialist system and try to undermine it. Taiwan is part of the sacred territory of the People's Republic of China. It is the lofty duty of the entire Chinese people, including our compatriots in Taiwan, to accomplish the great task of reunifying the motherland. In building socialism it is imperative to rely on the workers, peasants, and intellectuals and unite with all the forces that can be united. In the long years of revolution and construction, there has been formed under the leadership of the Communist Party of China a broad patriotic united front that is composed of democratic parties and people's organizations and embraces all socialist working people, all patriots who support socialism, and all patriots who stand for reunification of the motherland. This united front will continue to be consolidated and developed. The Chinese People's Political Consultative Conference is a broadly representative organization of the united front, which has played a significant historical role and will continue to do so in the political and social life of the country, in promoting friendship with the people of other countries, and in the struggle for socialist modernization and for the reunification and unity of the country. The People's Republic of China is a unitary multinational state built up jointly by the people of all its nationalities. Socialist relations of equality, unity, and mutual assistance have been established among them and will continue to be strengthened. In the struggle to safeguard the unity of the nationalities, it is necessary to combat big-nation chauvinism, mainly Han chauvinism, and also necessary to combat local-national chauvinism. The state does its utmost to promote the common prosperity of all nationalities in the country. China's achievements in revolution and construction are inseparable from support by the people of the world. The future of China is closely linked with that of the whole world. China adheres to an independent foreign policy as well as to the five principles of mutual respect for sovereignty and territorial integrity, mutual nonaggression, noninterference in each other's internal affairs, equality and mutual benefit, and peaceful coexistence in developing diplomatic relations and economic and cultural exchanges with other countries; China consistently opposes imperialism, hegemonism, and colonialism, works to strengthen unity with the people of other countries, supports the oppressed nations and the developing countries in their just struggle to win and preserve national independence and develop their national economies, and strives to safeguard world peace and promote the cause of human progress. This Constitution affirms the achievements of the struggles of the Chinese people of all nationalities and defines the basic system and basic tasks of the state in legal form; it is the fundamental law of the state and has supreme legal authority. The people of all nationalities, all state organs, the armed forces, all political parties and public organizations, and all enterprises and undertakings in the country must take the Constitution as the basic norm of conduct, and they have the duty to uphold the dignity of the Constitution and ensure its implementation.

CHAPTER 1: GENERAL PRINCIPLES

Article 1. The People's Republic of China is a socialist state under the people's democratic dictatorship led by the working class and based on the alliance of workers and peasants. The socialist system is the basic system of the People's Republic of China. Sabotage of the socialist system by any organization or individual is prohibited.

Article 2. All power in the People's Republic of China belongs to the people. The organs through which the people exercise state power are the National People's Congress and the local people's congresses at different levels. The people administer state affairs and manage economic, cultural, and social affairs through various channels and in various ways in accordance with the law.

Article 3. The state organs of the People's Republic of China apply the principle of democratic centralism. The National People's Congress and the local people's congresses at different levels are instituted through democratic election. They are responsible to the people and subject to their supervision. All administrative, judicial, and procuratorial organs of the state are created by the people's congresses to which they are responsible and under whose supervision they operate. The division of functions and powers between the central and local state organs is guided by the principle of giving full play to the initiative and enthusiasm of the local authorities under the unified leadership of the central authorities.

Article 4. All nationalities in the People's Republic of China are equal. The state protects the lawful rights and interests of the minority nationalities and upholds and develops the relationship of equality, unity, and mutual assistance among all of China's nationalities. Discrimination against and oppression of any nationality are prohibited; any acts that undermine the unity of the nationalities or instigate their secession are prohibited. The state helps the areas inhabited by minority nationalities speed up their economic and cultural development in accordance with the peculiarities and needs of the different minority nationalities. Regional autonomy is practiced in areas where people of minority nationalities live in compact communities; in these areas organs of self-government are established for the exercise of the right of autonomy. All the national autonomous areas are inalienable parts of the People's Republic of China. The people of all nationalities have the freedom to use and develop their own spoken and written languages and to preserve or reform their own ways and customs.

Article 5. The state upholds the uniformity and dignity of the socialist legal system. No law or administrative or local rules and regulations shall contravene the Constitution. All state organs, the armed forces, all political parties and public organizations, and all enterprises and undertakings must abide by the Constitution and the law. All acts in violation of the Constitution and the law must be investigated. No organization or individual may enjoy the privilege of being above the Constitution and the law.

Article 6. The basis of the socialist economic system of the People's Republic of China is socialist public ownership of the means of production, namely, ownership by the whole people and collective ownership by the working people. The system of socialist public ownership supersedes the system of exploitation of man by man; it applies the principle of "from each according to his ability, to each according to his work."

Article 7. The state economy is the sector of socialist economy under ownership by the whole people; it is the leading force in the national economy. The state ensures the consolidation and growth of the state economy.

Article 8. Rural people's communes, agricultural producers' cooperatives, and other forms of cooperative economy, such as producers' supply and marketing, credit and consumers' cooperatives, belong to the sector of socialist economy under collective ownership by the working people. Working people who are members of rural economic collectives have the right, within the limits prescribed by law, to farm private plots of cropland and hilly land, engage in household sideline production, and raise privately owned livestock. The various forms of cooperative economy in the cities and towns, such as those in the handicraft, industrial, building, transport, commercial, and service trades, all belong to the sector of socialist economy under collective ownership by the working people. The state protects the lawful rights and interests of the urban and rural economic collectives and encourages, guides, and helps the growth of the collective economy.

Article 9. Mineral resources, waters, forests, mountains, grassland, unreclaimed land, beaches, and other natural resources are owned by the state, that is, by the whole people, with the exception of the forests, mountains, grassland, unreclaimed land, and beaches that are owned by collectives in accordance with the law. The state ensures the rational use of natural resources and protects rare animals and plants. The appropriation or damage of natural resources by any organization or individual by whatever means is prohibited.

Article 10. Land in the cities is owned by the state. Land in the rural and suburban areas is owned by collectives except for those portions which belong to the state in accordance with the law; house sites and private plots of cropland and hilly land are also owned by collectives. The state may in the public interest take over land for its use in accordance with the law. No organization or individual may appropriate, buy, sell, or lease land, or unlawfully transfer land in other ways. All organizations and individuals who use land must make rational use of the land.

Article 11. The individual economy of urban and rural working people, operated within the limits prescribed by law, is a complement to the socialist public economy. The state protects the lawful rights and interests of the individual economy. The state guides, helps, and supervises the individual economy by exercising administrative control. The State permits the private economy to exist and develop within the limits prescribed by law. The private economy is a complement to the socialist public economy. The State protects the lawful rights and interests of the private economy, and guides, supervises, and administers the private economy.

Article 12. Socialist public property is sacred and inviolable. The state protects socialist public property. Appropriation or damage of state or collective property by any organization or individual by whatever means is prohibited.

Article 13. The state protects the right of citizens to own lawfully earned income, savings, houses, and other lawful property. The state protects by law the right of citizens to inherit private property.

Article 14. The state continuously raises labor productivity, improves economic results, and develops the productive forces by enhancing the enthusiasm of the working people, raising the level of their technical skill, disseminating advanced science and technology, improving the systems of economic administration and enterprise operation and management, instituting the socialist system of responsibility in various forms, and improving organization of work. The state practices strict economy and combats waste. The state properly apportions accumulation and consumption, pays attention to the interests of the collective and the individual as well as of the state and, on the basis of expanded production, gradually improves the material and cultural life of the people.

Article 15. The state practices economic planning on the basis of socialist public ownership. It ensures the proportionate and co-coordinated growth of the national economy through overall balancing by economic planning and the supplementary role of regulation by the market. Disturbance of the orderly functioning of the social economy or disruption of the state economic plan by any organization or individual is prohibited.

Article 16. State enterprises have decision-making power in operation and management within the limits prescribed by law, on condition that they submit to unified leadership by the state and fulfill all their obligations under the state plan. State enterprises practice democratic management through congresses of workers and staff and in other ways in accordance with the law.

Article 17. Collective economic organizations have decision-making power in conducting independent economic activities, on condition that they accept the guidance of the state plan and abide by the relevant laws. Collective economic organizations practice democratic management in accordance with the law, with the entire body of their workers electing or removing their managerial personnel and deciding on major issues concerning operation and management.

Article 18. The People's Republic of China permits foreign enterprises, other foreign economic organizations, and individual foreigners to invest in China and to enter into various forms of economic cooperation with Chinese enterprises and other economic organizations in accordance with the law of the People's Republic of China. All foreign enterprises and other foreign economic organizations in

China, as well as joint ventures with Chinese and foreign investment located in China, shall abide by the law of the People's Republic of China. Their lawful rights and interests are protected by the law of the People's Republic of China.

Article 19. The state develops socialist educational undertakings and works to raise the scientific and cultural level of the whole nation. The state runs schools of various types, makes primary education compulsory and universal, develops secondary, vocational, and higher education, and promotes preschool education. The state develops educational facilities of various types in order to wipe out illiteracy and provide political, cultural, scientific, technical, and professional education for workers, peasants, state functionaries, and other working people. It encourages people to become educated through self-study. The state encourages the collective economic organizations, state enterprises, and undertakings and other social forces to set up educational institutions of various types in accordance with the law. The state promotes the nationwide use of Putonghua [common speech based on Beijing pronunciation].

Article 20. The state promotes the development of the natural and social sciences, disseminates scientific and technical knowledge, and commends and rewards achievements in scientific research as well as technological discoveries and inventions.

Article 21. The state develops medical and health services, promotes modern medicine and traditional Chinese medicine, encourages and supports the setting up of various medical and health facilities by the rural economic collectives, state enterprises and undertakings, and neighborhood organizations, and promotes sanitation activities of a mass character, all to protect the people's health. The state develops physical culture and promotes mass sports activities to build up the people's physique.

Article 22. The state promotes the development of literature and art, the press, broadcasting and television undertakings, publishing and distribution services, libraries, museums, cultural centers, and other cultural undertakings that serve the people and socialism, and sponsors mass cultural activities. The state protects places of scenic and historical interest, valuable cultural monuments and relics, and other important items of China's historical and cultural heritage.

Article 23. The state trains specialized personnel in all fields who serve socialism, increases the number of intellectuals, and creates conditions to give full scope to their role in socialist modernization.

Article 24. The state strengthens the building of socialist spiritual civilization through spreading education in high ideals and morality, general education and education in discipline and the legal system, and through promoting the formulation and observance of rules of conduct and common pledges by different sections of the people in urban and rural areas. The state advocates the civic virtues of love for the motherland, for the people, for labor, for science, and for socialism; it educates the people in patriotism, collectivism, internationalism, and communism and in dialectical and historical materialism; it combats the decadent ideas of capitalism and feudalism and other decadent ideas.

Article 25. The state promotes family planning so that population growth may fit the plans for economic and social development.

Article 26. The state protects and improves the living environment and the ecological environment, and prevents and controls pollution and other public hazards. The state organizes and encourages forestation and the protection of forests.

Article 27. All state organs carry out the principle of simple and efficient administration, the system of responsibility for work, and the system of training functionaries and appraising their work in order constantly to improve quality of work and efficiency and combat bureaucratism. All state organs and functionaries must rely on the support of the people, keep in close touch with them, heed their opinions and suggestions, and accept their supervision and work hard to serve them.

Article 28. The state maintains public order and suppresses treasonable and other counterrevolutionary activities; it penalizes actions that endanger public security and disrupt the socialist economy and other criminal activities, and punishes and reforms criminals.

Article 29. The armed forces of the People's Republic of China belong to the people. Their tasks are to strengthen national defense, resist aggression, defend the motherland, safeguard the people's peaceful labor, participate in national reconstruction, and work hard to serve the people. The state strengthens the revolutionization, modernization, and regularization of the armed forces in order to increase the national defense capability.

Article 30. The administrative division of the People's Republic of China is as follows: (1) The country is divided into provinces, autonomous regions, and municipalities directly under the Central Government; (2) Provinces and autonomous regions are divided into autonomous prefectures, counties, autonomous counties, and cities; (3) Counties and autonomous counties are divided into townships, nationality townships, and towns. Municipalities directly under the Central Government and other large cities are divided into districts and counties. Autonomous prefectures are divided into counties, autonomous counties, and cities. All autonomous regions, autonomous prefectures, and autonomous counties are national autonomous areas.

Article 31. The state may establish special administrative regions when necessary. The systems to be instituted in special administrative regions shall be prescribed by law enacted by the National People's Congress in the light of the specific conditions.

Article 32. The People's Republic of China protects the lawful rights and interests of foreigners within Chinese territory, and while on Chinese territory foreigners must abide by the law of the People's Republic of China. The People's Republic of China may grant asylum to foreigners who request it for political reasons.

CHAPTER 2: THE FUNDAMENTAL RIGHTS AND DUTIES OF CITIZENS

Article 33. All persons holding the nationality of the People's Republic of China are citizens of the People's Republic of China. All citizens of the People's Republic of China are equal before the law. Every citizen enjoys the rights and at the same time must perform the duties prescribed by the Constitution and the law.

Article 34. All citizens of the People's Republic of China who have reached the age of eighteen have the right to vote and stand for election, regardless of nationality, race, sex, occupation, family background, religious belief, education, property status, or length of residence, except persons deprived of political rights according to law.

Article 35. Citizens of the People's Republic of China enjoy freedom of speech, of the press, of assembly, of association, of procession, and of demonstration.

Article 36. *Citizens of the People's Republic of China enjoy freedom of religious belief. No state organ, public organization, or individual may compel citizens to believe in, or not to believe in, any religion; nor may they discriminate against citizens who believe in, or do not believe in, any religion. The state protects normal religious activities. No one may make use of religion to engage in activities that disrupt public order, impair the health of citizens, or interfere with the educational system of the state. Religious bodies and religious affairs are not subject to any foreign domination.*

Article 37. The freedom of person of citizens of the People's Republic of China is inviolable. No citizen may be arrested except with the approval or by decision of a people's procuratorate or by decision of a people's court, and arrests must be made by a public security organ. Unlawful deprivation or restriction of citizens' freedom of person by detention or other means is prohibited; and unlawful search of the person of citizens is prohibited.

Article 38. The personal dignity of citizens of the People's Republic of China is inviolable. Insult, libel, false charge, or frame-up directed against citizens by any means is prohibited.

Article 39. The home of citizens of the People's Republic of China is inviolable. Unlawful search of, or intrusion into, a citizen's home is prohibited.

Article 40. The freedom and privacy of correspondence of citizens of the People's Republic of China are protected by law. No organization or individual may, on any ground, infringe upon the freedom and privacy of citizens' correspondence except in cases where, to meet the needs of state security or of investigation into criminal offenses, public security or procuratorial organs are permitted to censor correspondence in accordance with procedures prescribed by law.

Article 41. Citizens of the People's Republic of China have the right to criticize and make suggestions to any state organ or functionary. Citizens have the right to make to relevant state organs complaints and charges against, or exposures of, violation of the law or dereliction of duty by any state organ or functionary; but fabrication or distortion of facts with the intention of libel or frame-up is prohibited. In case of complaints, charges, or exposures made by citizens, the state organ concerned must deal with them in a responsible manner after ascertaining the facts. No one may suppress such complaints, charges, and exposures, or retaliate against the citizens making them. Citizens who have suffered losses through infringement of their civil rights by any state organ or functionary have the right to compensation in accordance with the law.

Article 42. Citizens of the People's Republic of China have the right as well as the duty to work. Using various channels, the state creates conditions for employment, strengthens labor protection, improves working conditions and, on the basis of expanded production, increases remuneration for work and social benefits. Work is the glorious duty of every able-bodied citizen. All working people in state enterprises and in urban and rural economic collectives should perform their tasks with an attitude consonant with their status as masters of the country. The state promotes socialist labor emulation, and commends and rewards model and advanced workers. The state encourages citizens to take part in voluntary labor. The state provides necessary vocational training to citizens before they are employed.

Article 43. Working people in the People's Republic of China have the right to rest. The state expands facilities for rest and recuperation of working people, and prescribes working hours and vacations for workers and staff.

Article 44. The state prescribes by law the system of retirement for workers and staff in enterprises and undertakings and for functionaries of organs of state. The livelihood of retired personnel is ensured by the state and society.

Article 45. Citizens of the People's Republic of China have the right to material assistance from the state and society when they are old, ill, or disabled. The state develops the social insurance, social relief, and medical and health services that are required to enable citizens to enjoy this right. The state and society ensure the livelihood of disabled members of the armed forces, provide pensions to the families of martyrs, and give preferential treatment to the families of military personnel. The state and society help make arrangements for the work, livelihood, and education of the blind, deaf-mute, and other handicapped citizens.

Article 46. Citizens of the People's Republic of China have the duty as well as the right to receive education. The state promotes the all-round moral, intellectual, and physical development of children and young people.

Article 47. Citizens of the People's Republic of China have the freedom to engage in scientific research, literary and artistic creation, and other cultural pursuits. The state encourages and assists creative endeavors conducive to the interests of the people made by citizens engaged in education, science, technology, literature, art, and other cultural work.

Article 48. Women in the People's Republic of China enjoy equal rights with men in all spheres of life, political, economic, cultural and social, and family life. The state protects the rights and interests of women, applies the principle of equal pay for equal work for men and women alike, and trains and selects cadres from among women.

Article 49. Marriage, the family, and mother and child are protected by the state. Both husband and wife have the duty to practice family planning. Parents have the duty to rear and educate their minor children, and children who have come of age have the duty to support and assist their parents. Violation of the freedom of marriage is prohibited. Maltreatment of old people, women, and children is prohibited.

Article 50. The People's Republic of China protects the legitimate rights and interests of Chinese nationals residing abroad and protects the lawful rights and interests of returned overseas Chinese and of the family members of Chinese nationals residing abroad.

Article 51. The exercise by citizens of the People's Republic of China of their freedoms and rights may not infringe upon the interests of the state, of society and of the collective, or upon the lawful freedoms and rights of other citizens.

Article 52. It is the duty of citizens of the People's Republic of China to safeguard the unity of the country and the unity of all its nationalities.

Article 53. Citizens of the People's Republic of China must abide by the Constitution and the law, keep state secrets, protect public property, and observe labor discipline and public order and respect social ethics.

Article 54. It is the duty of citizens of the People's Republic of China to safeguard the security, honor, and interests of the motherland; they must not commit acts detrimental to the security, honor, and interests of the motherland.

Article 55. It is the sacred obligation of every citizen of the People's Republic of China to defend the motherland and resist aggression. It is the honorable duty of citizens of the People's Republic of China to perform military service and join the militia in accordance with the law.

Article 56. It is the duty of citizens of the People's Republic of China to pay taxes in accordance with the law.

CHAPTER 3: THE STRUCTURE OF THE STATE

Section 1: The National People's Congress

Article 57. The National People's Congress of the People's Republic of China is the highest organ of state power. Its permanent body is the Standing Committee of the National People's Congress.

Article 58. The National People's Congress and its Standing Committee exercise the legislative power of the state.

Article 59. The National People's Congress is composed of deputies elected by the provinces, autonomous regions, and municipalities directly under the Central Government, and by the armed forces. All the minority nationalities are entitled to appropriate representation. Election of deputies to the National People's Congress is conducted by the Standing Committee of the National People's Congress. The number of deputies to the National People's Congress and the manner of their election are prescribed by law.

Article 60. The National People's Congress is elected for a term of five years. Two months before the expiration of the term of office of a National People's Congress, its Standing Committee must ensure that the election of deputies to the succeeding National People's Congress is completed. Should exceptional circumstances prevent such an election, it may be postponed by decision of a majority vote of more than two-thirds of all those on the Standing Committee of the incumbent National People's Congress, and the term of office of the incumbent National People's Congress may be extended. The election of deputies to the succeeding National People's Congress must be completed within one year after the termination of such exceptional circumstances.

Article 61. The National People's Congress meets in session once a year and is convened by its Standing Committee. A session of the National People's Congress may be convened at any time the Standing Committee deems this necessary, or when more than one-fifth of the deputies to the National People's Congress so propose. When the National People's Congress meets, it elects a presidium to conduct its session.

Article 62. The National People's Congress exercises the following functions and powers:

1. to amend the Constitution;
2. to supervise the enforcement of the Constitution;
3. to enact and amend basic statutes concerning criminal offenses, civil affairs, the state organs, and other matters;
4. to elect the President and the Vice-President of the People's Republic of China; *(previously translated as Chairman and Vice-Chairman of the People's Republic of China—translator's note.)*
5. to decide on the choice of the Premier of the State Council upon nomination by the President of the People's Republic of China, and to decide on the choice of the Vice-Premiers, State Councilors, Ministers in charge of Ministries or Commissions and the Auditor-General and the Secretary-General of the State Council upon nomination by the Premier;
6. to elect the Chairman of the Central Military Commission and, upon his nomination, to decide on the choice of the other members of the Central Military Commission;
7. to elect the President of the Supreme People's Court;
8. to elect the Procurator-General of the Supreme People's Procuratorate;
9. to examine and approve the plan for national economic and social development and the reports on its implementation;
10. to examine and approve the state budget and the report on its implementation;

11. to alter or annul inappropriate decisions of the Standing Committee of the National People's Congress;
12. to approve the establishment of provinces, autonomous regions, and municipalities directly under the Central Government;
13. to decide on the establishment of special administrative regions and the systems to be instituted there;
14. to decide on questions of war and peace; and
15. to exercise such other functions and powers as the highest organ of state power should exercise.

Article 63. The National People's Congress has the power to recall or remove from office the following persons:

1. the President and the Vice-President of the People's Republic of China;
2. the Premier, Vice-Premiers, State Councilors, Ministers in charge of Ministries or Commissions, and the Auditor-General and the Secretary-General of the State Council;
3. the Chairman of the Central Military Commission and others on the commission;
4. the President of the Supreme People's Court; and
5. the Procurator-General of the Supreme People's Procuratorate.

Article 64. Amendments to the Constitution are to be proposed by the Standing Committee of the National People's Congress or by more than one-fifth of the deputies to the National People's Congress and adopted by a majority vote of more than two-thirds of all the deputies to the Congress. Statutes and resolutions are adopted by a majority vote of more than one-half of all the deputies to the National People's Congress.

Article 65. The Standing Committee of the National People's Congress is composed of the following: the Chairman; the

Vice-Chairmen; the Secretary-General; and Members. Minority nationalities are entitled to appropriate representation on the Standing Committee of the National People's Congress. The National People's Congress elects, and has the power to recall, all those on its Standing Committee. No one on the Standing Committee of the National People's Congress shall hold any post in any of the administrative, judicial, or procuratorial organs of the state.

Article 66. The Standing Committee of the National People's Congress is elected for the same term as the National People's Congress; it exercises its functions and powers until a new Standing Committee is elected by the succeeding National People's Congress. The Chairman and Vice-Chairmen of the Standing Committee shall serve no more than two consecutive terms.

Article 67. The Standing Committee of the National People's Congress exercises the following functions and powers:

1. to interpret the Constitution and supervise its enforcement;
2. to enact and amend statutes with the exception of those which should be enacted by the National People's Congress;
3. to enact, when the National People's Congress is not in session, partial supplements and amendments to statutes enacted by the National People's Congress provided that they do not contravene the basic principles of these statutes;
4. to interpret statutes;
5. to examine and approve, when the National People's Congress is not in session, partial adjustments to the plan for national economic and social development and to the state budget that prove necessary in the course of their implementation;
6. to supervise the work of the State Council, the Central Military Commission, the Supreme People's Court, and the Supreme People's Procuratorate;
7. to annul those administrative rules and regulations, decisions or orders of the State Council that contravene the Constitution or the statutes;

8. to annul those local regulations or decisions of the organs of state power of provinces, autonomous regions, and municipalities directly under the Central Government that contravene the Constitution, the statutes, or the administrative rules and regulations;
9. to decide, when the National People's Congress is not in session, on the choice of Ministers in charge of Ministries or Commissions or the Auditor-General and the Secretary-General of the State Council upon nomination by the Premier of the State Council;
10. to decide, upon nomination by the Chairman of the Central Military Commission, on the choice of others on the commission, when the National People's Congress is not in session;
11. to appoint and remove the Vice-Presidents and judges of the Supreme People's Court, members of its Judicial Committee and the President of the Military Court at the suggestion of the President of the Supreme People's Court;
12. to appoint and remove the Deputy Procurators-General and procurators of the Supreme People's Procuratorate, members of its Procuratorial Committee and the Chief Procurator of the Military Procuratorate at the request of the Procurator-General of the Supreme People's Procuratorate, and to approve the appointment and removal of the chief procurators of the people's procuratorates of provinces, autonomous regions, and municipalities directly under the Central Government;
13. to decide on the appointment and recall of plenipotentiary representatives abroad;
14. to decide on the ratification and abrogation of treaties and important agreements concluded with foreign states;
15. to institute systems of titles and ranks for military and diplomatic personnel and of other specific titles and ranks;
16. to institute state medals and titles of honor and decide on their conferment;

17. to decide on the granting of special pardons;
18. to decide, when the National People's Congress is not in session, on the proclamation of a state of war in the event of an armed attack on the country or in fulfillment of international treaty obligations concerning common defense against aggression;
19. to decide on general mobilization or partial mobilization;
20. to decide on the enforcement of martial law throughout the country or in particular provinces, autonomous regions, or municipalities directly under the Central Government; and
21. to exercise such other functions and powers as the National People's Congress may assign to it.

Article 68. The Chairman of the Standing Committee of the National People's Congress presides over the work of the Standing Committee and convenes its meetings. The Vice-Chairmen and the Secretary-General assist the Chairman in his work. Chairmanship meetings with the participation of the Chairman, Vice-Chairmen and Secretary-General handle the important day-to-day work of the Standing Committee of the National People's Congress.

Article 69. The Standing Committee of the National People's Congress is responsible to the National People's Congress and reports on its work to the Congress.

Article 70. The National People's Congress establishes a Nationalities Committee, a Law Committee, a Finance and Economic Committee, an Education, Science, Culture and Public Health Committee, a Foreign Affairs Committee, an Overseas Chinese Committee, and such other special committees as are necessary. These special committees work under the direction of the Standing Committee of the National People's Congress when the Congress is not in session. The special committees examine, discuss, and draw up relevant bills and draft resolutions under the direction of the National People's Congress and its Standing Committee.

Article 71. The National People's Congress and its Standing Committee may, when they deem it necessary, appoint committees of inquiry into specific questions and adopt relevant resolutions in the light of their reports. All organs of state, public organizations, and citizens concerned are obliged to supply the necessary information to those committees of inquiry when they conduct investigations.

Article 72. Deputies to the National People's Congress and all those on its Standing Committee have the right, in accordance with procedures prescribed by law, to submit bills and proposals within the scope of the respective functions and powers of the National People's Congress and its Standing Committee.

Article 73. Deputies to the National People's Congress during its sessions, and all those on its Standing Committee during its meetings, have the right to address questions, in accordance with procedures prescribed by law, to the State Council or the ministries and commissions under the State Council, which must answer the questions in a responsible manner.

Article 74. No deputy to the National People's Congress may be arrested or placed on criminal trial without the consent of the Presidium of the current session of the National People's Congress or, when the National People's Congress is not in session, without the consent of its Standing Committee.

Article 75. Deputies to the National People's Congress may not be called to legal account for their speeches or votes at its meetings.

Article 76. Deputies to the National People's Congress must play an exemplary role in abiding by the Constitution and the law and keeping state secrets and, in production and other work and their public activities, assist in the enforcement of the Constitution and the law. Deputies to the National People's Congress should maintain close contact with the units and people which elected them, listen to and convey their opinions and demands, and work hard to serve them.

Article 77. Deputies to the National People's Congress are subject to the supervision of the units that elected them. The electoral units have the power, through procedures prescribed by law, to recall the deputies whom they elected.

Article 78. The organization and working procedures of the National People's Congress and its Standing Committee are prescribed by law.

Section 2: The President of the People's Republic of China

Article 79. The President and Vice-President of the People's Republic of China are elected by the National People's Congress. Citizens of the People's Republic of China who have the right to vote and to stand for election and who have reached the age of forty-five are eligible for election as President or Vice-President of the People's Republic of China. The term of office of the President and Vice-President of the People's Republic of China is the same as that of the National People's Congress, and they shall serve no more than two consecutive terms.

Article 80. The President of the People's Republic of China, in pursuance of decisions of the National People's Congress and its Standing Committee, promulgates statutes; appoints and removes the Premier, Vice-Premiers, State Councilors, Ministers in charge of Ministries or Commissions, and the Auditor-General and the Secretary-General of the State Council; confers state medals and titles of honor; issues orders of special pardons; proclaims martial law; proclaims a state of war; and issues mobilization orders.

Article 81. The President of the People's Republic of China receives foreign diplomatic representatives on behalf of the People's Republic of China and, in pursuance of decisions of the Standing Committee of the National People's Congress, appoints and recalls plenipotentiary representatives abroad, and ratifies and abrogates treaties and important agreements concluded with foreign states.

Article 82. The Vice-President of the People's Republic of China assists the President in his work. The Vice-President of the People's Republic of China may exercise such parts of the functions and powers of the President as the President may entrust to him.

Article 83. The President and Vice-President of the People's Republic of China exercise their functions and powers until the new President and Vice-President elected by the succeeding National People's Congress assume office.

Article 84. In case the office of the President of the People's Republic of China falls vacant, the Vice-President succeeds to the office of President. In case the office of the Vice-President of the People's Republic of China falls vacant, the National People's Congress shall elect a new Vice-President to fill the vacancy. In the event that the offices of both the President and the Vice-President of the People's Republic of China fall vacant, the National People's Congress shall elect a new President and a new Vice-President. Prior to such election, the Chairman of the Standing Committee of the National People's Congress shall temporarily act as the President of the People's Republic of China.

Section 3: The State Council

Article 85. The State Council, that is, the Central People's Government of the People's Republic of China, is the executive body of the highest organ of state power; it is the highest organ of state administration.

Article 86. The State Council is composed of the following: the Premier; the Vice-Premiers; the State Councilors; the Ministers in charge of Ministries; the Ministers in charge of Commissions; the Auditor-General; and the Secretary-General. The Premier has overall responsibility for the State Council. The Ministers have overall responsibility for the respective ministries or commissions under their charge. The organization of the State Council is prescribed by law.

Article 87. The term of office of the State Council is the same as that of the National People's Congress. The Premier, Vice-Premiers and State Councilors shall serve no more than two consecutive terms.

Article 88. The Premier directs the work of the State Council. The Vice-Premiers and State Councilors assist the Premier in his work.

Executive meetings of the State Council are composed of the Premier, the Vice-Premiers, the State Councilors and the Secretary-General of the State Council. The Premier convenes and presides over the executive meetings and plenary meetings of the State Council.

Article 89. The State Council exercises the following functions and powers: (1) to adopt administrative measures, enact administrative rules and regulations, and issue decisions and orders in accordance with the Constitution and the statutes; (2) to submit proposals to the National People's Congress or its Standing Committee; (3) to lay down the tasks and responsibilities of the ministries and commissions of the State Council, to exercise unified leadership over the work of the ministries and commissions, and to direct all other administrative work of a national character that does not fall within the jurisdiction of the ministries and commissions; (4) to exercise unified leadership over the work of local organs of state administration at different levels throughout the country, and to lay down the detailed division of functions and powers between the Central Government and the organs of state administration of provinces, autonomous regions, and municipalities directly under the Central Government; (5) to draw up and implement the plan for national economic and social development and the state budget; (6) to direct and administer economic work and urban and rural development; (7) to direct and administer the work concerning education, science, culture, public health, physical culture, and family planning; (8) to direct and administer the work concerning civil affairs, public security, judicial administration, supervision, and other related matters; (9) to conduct foreign affairs and conclude treaties and agreements with foreign states; (10) to direct and administer the building of national defense; (11) to direct and administer affairs concerning the nationalities and to safeguard the equal rights of minority nationalities and the right of autonomy of the national autonomous areas; (12) to protect the legitimate rights and interests of Chinese nationals residing abroad and protect the lawful rights and interests of returned overseas Chinese and of the family members of Chinese nationals residing abroad; (13) to alter or annul inappropriate orders, directives, and regulations issued by the ministries or commissions; (14) to alter or annul inappropriate decisions and orders issued by local organs of state administration at different levels; (15) to approve the geographic division of provinces, autonomous regions, and municipalities directly under the Central Government, and to approve the establishment and geographic division of autonomous prefectures, counties, autonomous counties and cities; (16) to decide on the enforcement of martial law in parts of provinces, autonomous regions and municipalities directly under the Central Government; (17) to examine and decide on the size of administrative organs and, in accordance with the law, to appoint, remove, and train administrative officers, appraise their work, and reward or punish them; and (18) to exercise such other functions and powers as the National People's Congress or its Standing Committee may assign it.

Article 90. The ministers in charge of ministries or commissions of the State Council are responsible for the work of their respective departments and convene and preside over their ministerial meetings or commission meetings that discuss and decide on major issues in the work of their respective departments. The ministries and commissions issue orders, directives, and regulations within the jurisdiction of their respective departments and in accordance with the statutes and the administrative rules and regulations, decisions, and orders issued by the State Council.

Article 91. The State Council establishes an auditing body to supervise through auditing the revenue and expenditure of all departments under the State Council and of the local governments at different levels, and those of the state financial and monetary organizations and of enterprises and undertakings. Under the direction of the Premier of the State Council, the auditing body independently exercises its power to supervise through auditing in accordance with the law, subject to no interference by any other administrative organ or any public organization or individual.

Article 92. The State Council is responsible, and reports on its work, to the National People's Congress or, when the National People's Congress is not in session, to its Standing Committee.

Section 4: The Central Military Commission

Article 93. The Central Military Commission of the People's Republic of China directs the armed forces of the country. The Central Military Commission is composed of the following: the Chairman; the Vice-Chairmen; and Members. The Chairman of the Central Military Commission has overall responsibility for the commission. The term of office of the Central Military Commission is the same as that of the National People's Congress.

Article 94. The Chairman of the Central Military Commission is responsible to the National People's Congress and its Standing Committee.

Section 5: The Local People's Congress and the Local People's Governments at Different Levels

Article 95. People's congresses and people's governments are established in provinces, municipalities directly under the Central Government, counties, cities, municipal districts, townships, nationality townships, and towns. The organization of local people's congresses and local people's governments at different levels is prescribed by law. Organs of self-government are established in autonomous regions, autonomous prefectures, and autonomous counties. The organization and working procedures of organs of self-government are prescribed by law in accordance with the basic principles laid down in Sections 5 and 6 of Chapter 3 of the Constitution.

Article 96. Local people's congresses at different levels are local organs of state power. Local people's congresses at and above the county level establish standing committees.

Article 97. Deputies to the people's congresses of provinces, municipalities directly under the Central Government, and cities divided into districts are elected by the people's congresses at the next lower level; deputies to the people's congresses of counties, cities not divided into districts, municipal districts, townships, nationality townships, and towns are elected directly by their constituencies. The number of deputies to local people's congresses at different levels and the manner of their election are prescribed by law.

Article 98. The term of office of the people's congresses of provinces, municipalities directly under the Central Government, and cities divided into districts is five years. The term of office of the people's congresses of counties, cities not divided into districts, municipal districts, townships, nationality townships, and towns is three years.

Article 99. Local people's congresses at different levels ensure the observance and implementation of the Constitution, the statutes, and the administrative rules and regulations in their respective administrative areas. Within the limits of their authority as prescribed by law, they adopt and issue resolutions and examine and decide on plans for local economic and cultural development and for development of public services. Local people's congresses at and above the county level examine and approve the plans for economic and social development and the budgets of their respective administrative areas, and examine and approve reports on their implementation. They have the power to alter or annul inappropriate decisions of their own standing committees. The people's congresses of nationality townships may, within the limits of their authority as prescribed by law, take specific measures suited to the peculiarities of the nationalities concerned.

Article 100. The people's congresses of provinces and municipalities directly under the Central Government, and their standing committees, may adopt local regulations that must not contravene the Constitution, the statutes, and the administrative rules and regulations, and they shall report such local regulations to the Standing Committee of the National People's Congress for the record.

Article 101. At their respective levels, local people's congresses elect, and have the power to recall, governors and deputy governors, or mayors and deputy mayors, or heads and deputy heads of counties, districts, townships, and towns. Local people's congresses at and above the county level elect, and have the power to recall, presidents of people's courts and chief procurators of people's procuratorates at the corresponding level. The election or recall of chief procurators of people's procuratorates shall be reported to the chief procurators of the people's procuratorates at the next higher level for submission to the standing committees of the people's congresses at the corresponding level for approval.

Article 102. Deputies to the people's congresses of provinces, municipalities directly under the Central Government, and cities divided into districts are subject to supervision by the units that elected them; deputies to the people's congresses of counties, cities not divided into districts, municipal districts, townships, nationality townships, and towns are subject to supervision by their constituencies. The electoral units and constituencies that elect deputies to local people's congresses at different levels have the power, according to procedures prescribed by law, to recall deputies whom they elected.

Article 103. The standing committee of a local people's congress at and above the county level is composed of a chairman, vice-chairmen, and members, and is responsible and reports on its work to the people's congress at the corresponding level. The local people's congress at and above the county level elects, and has the power to recall, anyone on the standing committee of the people's congress at the corresponding level. No one on the standing committee of a local people's congress at and above the county level shall hold any post in state administrative, judicial, and procuratorial organs.

Article 104. The standing committee of a local people's congress at and above the county level discusses and decides on major issues in all fields of work in its administrative area; supervises the work of the people's government, people's court, and people's procuratorate at the corresponding level; annuls inappropriate decisions and orders of the people's government at the corresponding level; annuls inappropriate resolutions of the people's congress at the next lower level; decides on the appointment and removal of functionaries of state organs within its jurisdiction as prescribed by law; and, when the people's congress at the corresponding level is not in session, recalls individual deputies to the people's congress at the next higher level and elects individual deputies to fill vacancies in that people's congress.

Article 105. Local people's governments at different levels are the executive bodies of local organs of state power as well as the local organs of state administration at the corresponding level. Local people's governments at different levels practice the system of overall responsibility by governors, mayors, county heads, district heads, township heads, and town heads.

Article 106. The term of office of local people's governments at different levels is the same as that of the people's congresses at the corresponding level.

Article 107. Local people's governments at and above the county level, within the limits of their authority as prescribed by law, conduct the administrative work concerning the economy, education, science, culture, public health, physical culture, urban and rural development, finance, civil affairs, public security, nationalities affairs, judicial administration, supervision, and family planning in their respective administrative areas; issue decisions and orders; appoint, remove, and train administrative functionaries, appraise their work, and reward or punish them. People's governments of townships, nationality townships, and towns carry out the resolutions of the people's congress at the corresponding level as well as the decisions and orders of the state administrative organs at the next higher level and conduct administrative work in their respective administrative areas. People's governments of provinces and municipalities directly under the Central Government decide on the establishment and geographic division of townships, nationality townships, and towns.

Article 108. Local people's governments at and above the county level direct the work of their subordinate departments and of people's governments at lower levels, and have the power to alter or annul inappropriate decisions of their subordinate departments and people's governments at lower levels.

Article 109. Auditing bodies are established by local people's governments at and above the county level. Local auditing bodies at different levels independently exercise their power to supervise through auditing in accordance with the law and are responsible to the people's government at the corresponding level and to the auditing body at the next higher level.

Article 110. Local people's governments at different levels are responsible and report on their work to people's congresses at the corresponding level. Local people's governments at and above the county level are responsible and report on their work to the standing committee of the people's congress at the corresponding level when the congress is not in session. Local people's governments at different levels are responsible and report on their work to the state administrative organs at the next higher level. Local people's governments at different levels throughout the country are state administrative organs under the unified leadership of the State Council and are subordinate to it.

Article 111. The residents' committees and villagers' committees established among urban and rural residents on the basis of their place of residence are mass organizations of self-management at the grass-roots level. The chairman, vice-chairmen, and members of each residents' or villagers' committee are elected by the residents. The relationship between the residents' and villagers' committees and the grass-roots organs of state power is prescribed by law. The residents' and villagers' committees establish committees for people's mediation, public security, public health, and other matters in order to manage public affairs and social services in their areas, mediate civil disputes, help maintain public order and convey residents' opinions and demands, and make suggestions to the people's government.

Section 6: The Organs of Self-Government of National Autonomous Areas

Article 112. The organs of self-government of national autonomous areas are the people's congresses and people's governments of autonomous regions, autonomous prefectures, and autonomous counties.

Article 113. In the people's congress of an autonomous region, prefecture, or county, in addition to the deputies of the nationality or nationalities exercising regional autonomy in the administrative area, the other nationalities inhabiting the area are also entitled to appropriate representation. The chairmanship and vice-chairmanships of the standing committee of the people's congress of an autonomous region, prefecture, or county shall include a citizen or citizens of the nationality or nationalities exercising regional autonomy in the area concerned.

Article 114. The administrative head of an autonomous region, prefecture, or county shall be a citizen of the nationality, or of one of the nationalities, exercising regional autonomy in the area concerned.

Article 115. The organs of self-government of autonomous regions, prefectures, and counties exercise the functions and powers of local organs of state as specified in Section 5 of Chapter 3 of the Constitution. At the same time, they exercise the right of autonomy within the limits of their authority as prescribed by the Constitution, the law of regional national autonomy, and other laws, and implement the laws and policies of the state in the light of the existing local situation.

Article 116. People's congresses of national autonomous areas have the power to enact autonomy regulations and specific regulations in the light of the political, economic, and cultural characteristics of the nationality or nationalities in the areas concerned. The autonomy regulations and specific regulations of autonomous regions shall be submitted to the Standing Committee of the National

People's Congress for approval before they go into effect. Those of autonomous prefectures and counties shall be submitted to the standing committees of the people's congresses of provinces or autonomous regions for approval before they go into effect, and they shall be reported to the Standing Committee of the National People's Congress for the record.

Article 117. The organs of self-government of the national autonomous areas have the power of autonomy in administering the finances of their areas. All revenues accruing to the national autonomous areas under the financial system of the state shall be managed and used independently by the organs of self-government of those areas.

Article 118. The organs of self-government of the national autonomous areas independently arrange for and administer local economic development under the guidance of state plans. In developing natural resources and building enterprises in the national autonomous areas, the state shall give due consideration to the interests of those areas.

Article 119. The organs of self-government of the national autonomous areas independently administer educational, scientific, cultural, public health, and physical culture affairs in their respective areas, sort out and protect the cultural legacy of the nationalities, and work for the development and prosperity of their cultures.

Article 120. The organs of self-government of the national autonomous areas may, in accordance with the military system of the state and concrete local needs and with the approval of the State Council, organize local public security forces for the maintenance of public order.

Article 121. In performing their functions, the organs of self-government of the national autonomous areas, in accordance with the autonomy regulations of the respective areas, employ the spoken and written language or languages in common use in the locality.

Article 122. The state gives financial, material, and technical assistance to the minority nationalities to accelerate their economic and cultural development. The state helps the national autonomous areas train large numbers of cadres at different levels and specialized personnel and skilled workers of different professions and trades from among the nationality or nationalities in those areas.

Section 7: The People's Court and the People's Procuratorates

Article 123. The people's courts in the People's Republic of China are the judicial organs of the state.

Article 124. The People's Republic of China establishes the Supreme People's Court and the local people's courts at different levels, military courts, and other special people's courts. The term of office of the President of the Supreme People's Court is the same as that of the National People's Congress; he shall serve no more than two consecutive terms. The organization of people's courts is prescribed by law.

Article 125. All cases handled by the people's courts, except for those involving special circumstances as specified by law, shall be heard in public. The accused has the right of defense.

Article 126. The people's courts shall, in accordance with the law, exercise judicial power independently and are not subject to interference by administrative organs, public organizations, or individuals.

Article 127. The Supreme People's Court is the highest judicial organ. The Supreme People's Court supervises the administration of justice by the local people's courts at different levels and by the special people's courts; people's courts at higher levels supervise the administration of justice by those at lower levels.

Article 128. The Supreme People's Court is responsible to the National People's Congress and its Standing Committee. Local people's courts at different levels are responsible to the organs of state power that created them.

Article 129. The people's procuratorates of the People's Republic of China are state organs for legal supervision.

Article 130. The People's Republic of China establishes the Supreme People's Procuratorate and the local people's procuratorates at different levels, military procuratorates, and other special people's procuratorates. The term of office of the Procurator-General of the Supreme People's Procuratorate is the same as that of the National People's Congress; he shall serve no more than two consecutive terms. The organization of people's procuratorates is prescribed by law.

Article 131. People's procuratorates shall, in accordance with the law, exercise procuratorial power independently and are not subject to interference by administrative organs, public organizations, or individuals.

Article 132. The Supreme People's Procuratorate is the highest procuratorial organ. The Supreme People's Procuratorate directs the work of the local people's procuratorates at different levels and of the special people's procuratorates; people's procuratorates at higher levels direct the work of those at lower levels.

*Article 133.*The Supreme People's Procuratorate is responsible to the National People's Congress and its Standing Committee. Local people's procuratorates at different levels are responsible to the organs of state power at the corresponding levels that created them and to the people's procuratorates at the higher level.

Article 134. Citizens of all nationalities have the right to use the spoken and written languages of their own nationalities in court proceedings. The people's courts and people's procuratorates should provide translation for any party to the court proceedings who is not familiar with the spoken or written languages in common use in the locality. In an area where people of a minority nationality live in a compact community or where a number of nationalities live together, hearings should be conducted in the language or languages in common use in the locality; indictments, judgments, notices, and other documents should be written, according to actual needs, in the language or languages in common use in the locality.

Article 135. The people's courts, people's procuratorates, and public security organs shall, in handling criminal cases, divide their functions, each taking responsibility for its own work, and they shall coordinate their efforts and check each other to ensure correct and effective enforcement of law.

CHAPTER 4: THE NATIONAL FLAG, THE NATIONAL EMBLEM, AND THE CAPITAL

Article 136. The national flag of the People's Republic of China is a red flag with five stars.

Article 137. The national emblem of the People's Republic of China is Tian'anmen in the center illuminated by five stars and encircled by ears of grain and a cogwheel.

Article 138. The capital of the People's Republic of China is Beijing.

Amendment One

(Approved on April 12, 1988 by the Seventh NPC at its First Session)

1. Article 11 of the Constitution shall include a new paragraph, which reads: "The State permits the private sector of the economy to exist and develop within the limits prescribed by law. The private sector of the economy is a complement to the socialist public economy. The State protects the lawful rights and interests of the private sector of the economy and exercises guidance, supervision, and control over the private sector of the economy."
2. The fourth sentence of Article 10 of the Constitution, which provides that "no organization or individual may appropriate, buy, sell, or lease land or otherwise engage in the transfer of land by unlawful means," shall be amended as: "no organization or individual may appropriate, buy, sell, or otherwise

engage in the transfer of land by unlawful means. The right to the use of land may be transferred according to law."

Amendment Two

(Approved on March 29, 1993 by the Eighth NPC at its First Session)

3. The last two sentences of the seventh paragraph of the Preamble, which reads, "The basic task of the nation in the years to come is to concentrate its effort on socialist modernization. Under the leadership of the Communist Party of China and the guidance of Marxism-Leninism and Mao Zedong Thought, the Chinese people of all nationalities will continue to adhere to the people's democratic dictatorship and follow the socialist road, steadily improve socialist institutions, develop socialist democracy, improve the socialist legal system and work hard and self-reliantly to modernize industry, agriculture, national defense, and science and technology step by step to turn China into a socialist country with a high level of culture and democracy," shall be amended as: "China is at the primary stage of socialism. The basic task of the nation is, according to the theory of building socialism with Chinese characteristics, to concentrate its effort on socialist modernization. Under the leadership of the Communist Party of China and the guidance of Marxism-Leninism and Mao Zedong Thought, the Chinese people of all nationalities will continue to adhere to the people's democratic dictatorship and follow the socialist road, persevere in reform and opening to the outside, steadily improve socialist institutions, develop socialist democracy, improve the socialist legal system, and work hard and self-reliantly to modernize industry, agriculture, national defense, and science and technology step by step to turn China into a socialist country with prosperity and power, democracy and culture."

4. At the end of the tenth paragraph of the Preamble, add "The system of multi-party cooperation and political consultation led by the Communist Party of China will exist and develop in China for a long time to come."
5. Article 7, which reads, "The state economy is the sector of socialist economy under ownership by the whole people; it is the leading force in the national economy. The state ensures the consolidation and growth of the state economy," shall be changed to: "The state-owned economy, that is, the socialist economy under ownership by the whole people, is the leading force in the national economy. The state ensures the consolidation and growth of the state-owned economy."
6. The first item of Article 8, which reads, "Rural people's communes, agricultural producers' cooperatives, and other forms of cooperative economy such as producers' supply and marketing, credit and consumers' cooperatives, belong to the sector of socialist economy under collective ownership by the working people. Working people who are members of rural economic collectives have the right, within the limits prescribed by law, to farm plots of cropland and hilly land allotted for private use, engage in household sideline production, and raise privately-owned livestock," shall be amended as: "Rural household-based contract responsibility system with remuneration linked to output, and other forms of cooperative economy such as producers' supply and marketing, credit and consumers' cooperatives, belong to the sector of socialist economy under collective ownership by the working people. Working people who are members of rural economic collectives have the right, within the limits prescribed by law, to farm plots of cropland and hilly land allotted for private use, engage in household sideline production, and raise privately-owned livestock."
7. Article 15, which reads, "The state practices economic planning on the basis of socialist public ownership. It ensures

the proportionate and coordinated growth of the national economy through overall balancing by economic planning and the supplementary role of regulation by the market. Disturbance of the orderly functioning of the social economy or disruption of the state economic plan by any organization or individual is prohibited," shall be changed to: "The state has put into practice a socialist market economy. The state strengthens formulating economic laws, improves macro adjustment and control, and forbids according to law any units or individuals from interfering with the social economic order."

8. Article 16, which reads, "State enterprises have decision-making power in operation and management within the limits prescribed by law, on condition that they submit to unified leadership by the state and fulfill their obligations under the state plan. State enterprises practice democratic management through congresses of workers and staff and in other ways in accordance with the law," shall be revised as: "State-owned enterprises have decision-making power in operation and management within the limits prescribed by law. State-owned enterprises practice democratic management through congresses of workers and staff and in other ways in accordance with the law."
9. Article 17, which reads, "Collective economic organizations have decision-making power in conducting independent economic activities, on condition that they accept the guidance of the state plan and abide by the relevant laws. Collective economic organizations practice democratic management in accordance with the law, with the entire body of their workers electing or removing their managerial personnel and deciding on major issues concerning operation and management," shall be amended as: "Collective economic organizations have decision-making power in conducting independent economic activities, on condition that they abide by the relevant

laws. Collective economic organizations practice democratic management, elect or remove their managerial personnel, and decide on major issues concerning operation and management according to law."

10. The item of Article 42 which reads "Work is the glorious duty of every able-bodied citizen. All working people in state enterprises and in urban and rural economic collectives should perform their tasks with an attitude consonant with their status as masters of the country. The state promotes socialist labor emulation and commends and rewards model and advanced workers. The state encourages citizens to take part in voluntary labor," shall be amended as: "Work is the glorious duty of every able-bodied citizen. All working people in state-owned enterprises and in urban and rural economic collectives should perform their tasks with an attitude consonant with their status as masters of the country. The state promotes socialist labor emulation and commends and rewards model and advanced workers. The state encourages citizens to take part in voluntary labor."
11. Article 98, which reads, "The term of office of the people's congresses of provinces, municipalities directly under the Central Government, and cities divided into districts is five years. The term of office of the people's congresses of countries, cities not divided into districts, municipal districts, townships, nationality townships, and towns is three years," shall be revised as: "The term of office of the people's congresses of provinces, municipalities directly under the Central Government, counties, cities, and municipal districts is five years. The term of office of the people's congresses of townships, nationality townships, and towns is three years."

Amendment Three

(Approved on March 15, 1999 by the Ninth NPC at its Second Session)

The original text of paragraph seven in the Preamble of the Constitution is: "Both the victory of China's new-democratic revolution and the successes of its socialist cause have been achieved by the Chinese people of all nationalities under the leadership of the Communist Party of China and the guidance of Marxism-Leninism and Mao Zedong Thought, and by upholding truth, correcting errors, and overcoming numerous difficulties and hardships. China is currently in the primary stage of socialism. The basic task of the nation is to concentrate its effort on socialist modernization in accordance with the theory of building socialism with Chinese characteristics. Under the leadership of the Communist Party of China and the guidance of Marxism-Leninism and Mao Zedong Thought, the Chinese people of all nationalities will continue to adhere to the people's democratic dictatorship, follow the socialist road, persist in reform and opening-up, steadily improve socialist institutions, develop socialist democracy, improve the socialist legal system, and work hard and self-reliantly to modernize industry, agriculture, national defense, and science and technology step by step to turn China into a powerful and prosperous socialist country with a high level of culture and democracy."

It is revised into: "Both the victory of China's new-democratic revolution and the successes of its socialist cause have been achieved by the Chinese people of all nationalities under the leadership of the Communist Party of China and the guidance of Marxism-Leninism and Mao Zedong Thought, and by upholding truth, correcting errors, and overcoming numerous difficulties and hardships. China will stay in the primary stage of socialism for a long period of time. The basic task of the nation is to concentrate its efforts on socialist modernization by following the road of building socialism with Chinese characteristics. Under the leadership of the Communist Party of China and the guidance of Marxism-Leninism, Mao Zedong Thought and Deng Xiaoping Theory, the Chinese people of all nationalities will continue to adhere to the people's democratic dictatorship, follow the socialist road, persist in reform and opening-up, steadily improve socialist institutions, develop a socialist market economy, advance socialist democracy, improve the socialist legal system, and work hard and self-reliantly to modernize industry, agriculture, national defense, and science and technology step by step to turn China into a powerful and prosperous socialist country with a high level of culture and democracy."

One section is added to Article 5 of the Constitution as the first section: "The People's Republic of China practices ruling the country in accordance with the law and building a socialist country of law."

The original text of Article 6 of the Constitution is: "The basis of the socialist economic system of the People's Republic of China is socialist public ownership of the means of production, namely, ownership by the whole people and collective ownership by the working people. The system of socialist public ownership supersedes the system of exploitation of man by man; it applies the principle of 'from each according to his ability, to each according to his work.'"

It is revised into: "The basis of the socialist economic system of the People's Republic of China is socialist public ownership of the means of production, namely, ownership by the whole people and collective ownership by the working people. The system of socialist public ownership supersedes the system of exploitation of man by man; it applies the principle of 'from each according to his ability, to each according to his work.' During the primary stage of socialism, the state adheres to the basic economic system with the public ownership remaining dominant and diverse sectors of the economy developing side by side, and to the distribution system with the distribution according to work remaining dominant and the coexistence of a variety of modes of distribution."

The original text of the first section in Article 8 of the Constitution is: "The rural household-based output-related contracted responsibility system and other forms of the cooperative economy such as producers' supply and marketing, credit and consumers' cooperatives, belong to the sector of the socialist economy under collective ownership by the working people. Working people who are members of rural economic collectives have the right, within the limits prescribed by law, to farm plots of cropland and hilly land allotted for private use, engage in household sideline production, and raise privately owned livestock."

It is revised into: "Rural collective economic organizations practice the double-tier management system that combines unified and separate operations on the basis of the household-based output-related contracted responsibility system. Various forms of the cooperative economy in rural areas such as producers', supply and marketing, credit and consumers' cooperatives belong to the sector of the socialist economy under collective ownership by the working people. Working people who are members of rural economic collectives have the right, within the limits prescribed by law, to farm plots of cropland and hilly land allotted for private use, engage in household sideline production, and raise privately owned livestock."

The original text of Article 11 of the Constitution is: "The individual economy of urban and rural working people, operated within the limits prescribed by law, is a complement to the socialist public economy. The state protects the lawful rights and interests of the individual economy. The state guides, helps, and supervises the individual economy by exercising administrative control. The state permits the private economy to exist and develop within the limits prescribed by law. The private economy is a complement to the socialist public economy. The state protects the lawful rights and interests of the private economy, and guides, supervises, and administers the private economy."

It is revised into: "Individual, private, and other nonpublic economies that exist within the limits prescribed by law are major components of the socialist market economy. The state protects the lawful rights and interests of individual and private economies, and guides, supervises, and administers individual and private economies."

The original text of Article 28 of the Constitution is: "The state maintains public order and suppresses treasonable and other counterrevolutionary activities; it penalizes actions that endanger public security and disrupt the socialist economy and other criminal activities, and punishes and reforms criminals."

It is revised into: "The state maintains public order and suppresses treasonable and other criminal activities that endanger state security; it penalizes actions that endanger public security and disrupt the socialist economy and other criminal activities, and punishes and reforms criminals." (Updated in 1999)

Selected Bibliography

Adeney, David H. *China: The Church's Long March.* Ventura, CA: Regal Books, 1985.

Bonhoeffer, Dietrich. *The Cost of Discipleship.* New York: Simon & Schuster, 1995.

Brown, G. Thompson. *Christianity in the People's Republic of China.* Atlanta: John Knox Press, 1983.

de Bary, William Theodore, ed. *Sources of Chinese Tradition.* New York: Columbia University Press, 1960.

Dumas, Alexandre. *The Count of Monte Cristo.* New York: Bantam Books, 1956.

Fraser, John. *The Chinese.* New York: Summit Books, 1980.

Garraty, John A. *The Columbia History of the World.* New York: Harper & Row, 1972.

Graham, Franklin. *Bob Pierce, This One Thing I Do.* Waco, TX: Word Books, 1983.

Hitchcock, James. *Catholicism and Modernity.* New York: The Seabury Press, 1979.

Jung Chang and Joh Halliday. *Mao: the unknown story.* New York: Random House, 2005.

Kane, Herbert. *A Global View of Christian Missions.* Grand Rapids: Baker Book House, 1985.

Karnow, Stanley. *Mao and China: A Legacy of Turmoil.* New York: Penguin Books, 1985.

Latourette, Kenneth Scott. *A History of Christianity.* New York: Harper & Brothers, 1953.

Li, Xinyuan. *Theological Construction—or Destruction.* Streamwood, IL: Christian Life Press, 1997.

Li, Zhisui. *The Private Life of Chairman Mao.* New York: Random House, 1994.

Malek, Roman. *Monumenta Serica Monograh Series L1.* Nettetal: Styler Verlag, 2002.

Nien, Cheng. *Life and Death in Shanghai.* New York: Penguin Books, 1988.

Pott, F. L. Hawks. *A Sketch of Chinese History.* Shanghai: Kelly and Walsh, 1923.

Reeves, Thomas. *The Empty Church: The Suicide of Liberal Christianity.* New York: The Free Press, 1997.

Rittenberg, Sydney. *The Man Who Stayed Behind.* New York: Simon & Schuster, 1993.

Skinner, Betty Lee. *Daws.* Grand Rapids, MI: The Zondervan Corporation, 1974.

The Holy Bible. King James Version.

Ting, K. H. *Adjustment of Theological Thinking.* Shanghai: Tian Feng 4, 2000.

Ting, K. H. *Love Never Ends.* Nanjing: Nanjing Amity Printing Co., Ltd., 1998.

Twitchell, Ken. *Dare to be Different.* Reading: Christian Focus Publication, 2004.

Wickeri, Philip. *Seeking the Common Ground.* Maryknoll, NY: Orbis Books, 1988.

Index

D

E

F

G

H

I

J

K

L

T

V

W

Y

Z

Endorsements

It is fitting that a son of pioneer missionaries to China, himself deeply involved in the contemporary Christian movement in that great nation, should give a brilliant answer to the discussion swirling around the issue of the unregistered house church movement and the registered Three-Self Church. Dr. Bürklin's careful historical analysis of pre-Communist China, taking us back hundreds of years, also reveals a characteristic of Chinese culture that allows a more balanced view of government-church relations. At the same time this book will excite in the hearts of sincere Christians the glorious prospect of the church in China becoming the great sending church of this century.

Along with careful scholarship we find beautiful and profoundly challenging biographical sketches of Christian heroes, such as Wang Mingdao, exposing the surface Christianity typical of so much of our more affluent Western Christianity and calling us in the West to a radical evaluation of our own discipleship and a fresh commitment to Christ as Lord of all.

Ian North, Founder, Ambassadors for Christ India, Sydney, Australia

Dr. Werner Bürklin is a friend of the Chinese Church. His love for China and his passion for training Christian workers are evidenced by his frequently traveling to China and conducting seminars on evangelism and pastoral care. His firsthand experience and wide exposure make his writing and the story he tells credible, balanced, and worth reading.

Dr. Wilson W. Chow, President, China Graduate School of Theology, Hong Kong, China

I hope this important book is read by all who care about the cause of the gospel in China. Dr. Bürklin draws on his rich personal history of partnering with Chinese Christians—especially those in the registered churches—to dispel the myths and misperceptions that have kept many of us in the West from celebrating the wonderful things that God is doing in that great country.

Dr. Richard J. Mouw, President and Professor of Christian Philosophy Fuller Theological Seminary, Pasadena, California, USA

Hardly anyone in the evangelical world knows China better than Werner Bürklin. Read this book to gain a perspective on the church of Jesus Christ in China today—and how it got there— that you will find nowhere else. He shares his knowledge of the history, personalities, sufferings, movements, theologies, and challenges facing the future in a most eye-opening manner.

Dr. John A. Huffman, Senior Pastor, St. Andrews Presbyterian Church New Port Beach, California, USA

Jesus Never Left China should be mandatory reading for every Christian. This is a truly inside picture of God's most exciting building site on earth today.

Dr. Wilfried Reuter, Director Emeritus, Rüstzentrum Krelingen, Germany

Having traveled extensively and regularly with Dr. Bürklin throughout China since 1991, I am of the firm opinion that "the rest of the story" concerning the church in China needs to be told.

His book will fill important gaps in the many selective reports that come out of China as to how God has been moving in the church there over recent years.

Wilbur Wright, Auckland, New Zealand

What God is doing today in China is one of the most amazing stories in world history. The former country of Mao Zedong is today the center of a spiritual revival in the world. Dr. Werner Bürklin writes as an insider. His parents had to leave China after the communist revolution. But Jesus never left China! This book will be the textbook for modern mission history in China. Take it, read it, and be amazed.

Dr. Stephan Holthaus, Academic Dean, Freie Theologische Akademie, Gießen, Germany

Much has been written about China. What I consider so special about Dr. Werner Bürklin is his personal history with this country and people, and the way God led him to encourage Christians in China and all over the world to be part of God's history in this huge land—independent from clichés among evangelicals and liberals. China remains complex—but the footprints of Jesus are clearly seen by those who are ready to be surprised by God's history. Werner Bürklin is competent to reveal parts of it—and even more important—he is full of God's love for the people in China.

Martin Voegelin, Director, Arbeitsgemenschaft Evangelikaler Missionen, Zürich, Switzerland

Werner Bürklin was born in China and came to faith there, and so it is no surprise that China is in his blood. He knows the country, its people, and the church better than most and writes with deep intensity and compassion about the needs, the challenges, and the opportunities facing the people of God in the most populous nation on earth.

Dr. Stuart Briscoe, International Bible Teacher, Author of Brave Enough to Follow

Dr. Bürklin writes with a unique passion, combining both his love for the land of his birth and his love for the church of Christ. He brings rationality, clarity, and understanding to a subject that, in the Western world and church, is mostly misunderstood and confused. This well-written and extremely readable book is a must for those who want a fuller understanding of the roots of today's church in China.

Terry Calkin, Senior Pastor, Greenlane Christian Centre, Auckland, New Zealand

Dr. Bürklin's book is highly informative and levelheaded in its historical assessments but also emotionally moving and spiritually illuminating.

Dr. Manfred Siebald, University of Mainz, Germany

Few of us born in China in the early 20th century are still alive—Werner is one of them. He always endeavored to paint a true picture of God's mighty work in China and succeeded again. Read this book and be blessed.

Ruth Graham, Montreat, NC, USA

To order additional copies of

JESUS NEVER LEFT CHINA

The Rest of the Story

Have your credit card ready and call:

1-877-421-READ (7323)

or please visit our web site at
www.pleasantword.com

Also available at:
www.amazon.com
and
www.barnesandnoble.com